The Girl That No One Claimed:

When Hell Comes Back

By: P. Johnson

Copyright

The Girl That No One Claimed: When Hell Comes Back

No part of this publication may be reproduced or transmitted in any form or by any means, electronic or mechanical, including photocopy, recording, scanning, or any information storage and retrieval system, without written permission from the publisher/author, except for brief quotations used in reviews.

Content Note

This book contains depictions and discussions of domestic abuse, coercive control, sexual assault, and trauma. Please take care of yourself while reading and pause as needed.

Disclaimer

This book is a memoir based on the author's life.

Names, locations, identifying details, and certain events have been altered in places to protect privacy and for narrative clarity. Any similarity to persons or events not intended by the author is coincidental.

Nothing in this book is intended as legal, medical, or professional advice.

Author Note

$\mathcal{I}$ wrote this to keep the focus where it belongs: on what happens inside a person when love, fear, and survival get tangled. It's written to show how my childhood in *The Girl That No One Claimed* has echoed into adult life, and how the past doesn't just disappear because time passes. Some of the chapters move fast because memory isn't linear. Some chapters get heavier because that's how those days felt—heavy. If you have Lived through trauma, or you love someone who has, I wrote this for you. If you haven't, I hope this helps you understand the parts people don't talk about. Most of all, if any part of this feels like you, I want you to feel seen— without having to explain yourself.

Content

Table of Contents

*For everyone who learned to keep walking even
when life never bothered to clear the path.*

CHAPTER ONE

One Down, One to Go

***

It was the summer, right after graduation.

Revenge didn't show up the way movies promise. There wasn't a thunderstorm or a slammed door in slow motion.
No swelling soundtrack while I delivered a speech that changed my life.

Mine started with overcooked food and a woman who thought her sons pissed holy water.

It was just a sentence thrown at me across a kitchen table in a group home.

The kitchen was always too bright. Fluorescent light bounced off cheap countertops like it was trying to expose everything in me. It smelled like overcooked food, dish soap, and whatever frustration she'd been marinating in all day. Utensils scraped. A glass clinked. Ordinary sounds turned into warnings in that room.

She didn't have to shout to control it. She spoke calmly, like a weather reporter, and everyone's body adjusted around her words.

That's what I remember most: my chest tightening before she even finished the sentence. My body already knew the rule. Love was something other people got. I was supposed to be grateful for leftovers.

My group-home foster mom loved reminding me exactly where she thought I belonged. She had sons—

grown, single, the pride of her life—and whenever they came up, she twisted the knife just enough to make it land.

"They would never be with a girl like you," she said.
"They wouldn't even give you the time of day. You'd never meet their standards."

She didn't say it like she was being cruel.
She said it like she was reading a forecast:
Chance of low self-esteem, with a ninety-eight percent likelihood you die alone.

I was expected to nod. To be grateful she let me breathe under her roof at all.

That sentence didn't make me sad.
It made something lock into place.

I didn't hear it as a warning. I heard it as a rule.
And rules, were only real if you followed them.

This wasn't empowerment.
It was pain taking control.

At the time, control felt close enough to safe and at that time I couldn't tell the difference.

I was the girl who should be thankful for a bed. For food. For rules that shifted with her moods. Her sons, though? That was premium-level life—the kind of stability I was never meant to touch.

So I made a quiet pact with myself.

One day, I was going to prove she didn't know her sons as well as she thought she did.

Back then, I couldn't do anything about it. I was still under their roof, under the system, under everyone's thumb. But the phrase stayed lodged in my chest like a splinter:

A girl like you.

Fine. A girl like me would wait.

When I finally got out and started standing on my own two feet, that splinter turned into a plan.

Her "baby boy" wasn't a baby anymore. He was in his late twenties—full-grown, and very much the golden child she held up as the standard I could never reach.

Let me be clear: I wasn't someone who just slept with everyone. I'd learned early that my body was more bargaining chip than sacred temple, and nobody else was protecting it. So when I said yes, it was for a reason.

This wasn't random.
It was targeted—pain dressed up as intention.

I didn't come at him drunk or sloppy. I didn't throw myself across his lap at a party. I just started talking to him. Showing up where he was. Making sure he saw me, not the charity-case version his mother had narrated for years.

We flirted. We joked. Conversations ran later than they should have. That low, steady current was there, and I knew it.

When it finally happened, it wasn't dramatic. Just two sober adults crossing a line we'd both been pretending wasn't there.

The next morning, he was nervous. Over-explaining. Talking about how young I was. How he didn't want me to "get attached." How he wasn't looking for anything serious and didn't want to hurt me.

He talked to me like I was some fragile girl who'd confuse sex with a love story and start doodling his last name in a notebook.

The whole time, I sat there thinking:

Baby, you are not that special.

He thought he was letting me down gently. Like he was the main character and I was about to sob into a pillow over losing my shot at being Mrs. Golden Boy.

I almost laughed.

Instead, I smiled. Told him I understood. Hit him with the cool, calm "no worries" like he'd canceled coffee, not some imaginary future I never wanted. I grabbed my clothes, got dressed, and walked out with a smile like I'd just closed a deal.

Inside, the thought was simple:

One down. One to go.

I convinced myself it was closure.
It wasn't. It was me keeping score.

A couple months later, I pulled into the group-home driveway again.

This time, I wasn't the girl living there.
I was the woman pulling up in her own car, on her own terms.

I did that "I was just stopping by" *look how well I'm doing now* visit.

But I knew exactly what I was looking for.

Son number two.

The second trophy she swore I could never even get a glance from.

He was staying in a camper in her yard, like some sad bonus level waiting to be unlocked.

I walked into the house like I was grateful. Like I was the good former foster kid coming back to say thank you for everything she'd done. I smiled. I nodded. I played the part.

We sat at the same table where she'd once told me her sons were out of my league.

I didn't waste time.

I told her I wasn't staying long and asked about him—why he was living out there instead of the perfect life she used to brag about.

She launched right into it.

His ex had thrown him out. He was "healing." Staying close while he got himself together. She laid his whole situation out for me like a menu: heartbroken, displaced, vulnerable.

In my head, a small, cold voice went:

Hmm. Weak and easy.

She kept talking—his pain, his mistakes, his journey. I nodded, tilting my head just right, playing the understanding visitor.

When she finished, I stood up, hugged her, and walked straight out the door.

Not to my car, to his camper.
Just like with her first son, it wasn't sloppy. No alcohol. No lost-girl act. Just two sober adults feeling out the edges of something we both knew we shouldn't be touching.

That night, I came back.

Both of us knowing exactly what we were doing.

I got number two.

The next morning, she woke up to my car in her driveway and me stepping out of her son's camper.

No shame.

It wasn't right, but anger has a way of rewriting ethics when it's been starving too long.

She came outside, squinting into the daylight, confusion fighting with recognition.

I looked her straight in the eye and said, calm and clear,

"I guess you don't know your sons very well."

Her face twisted—shock, anger, the math trying to load.

"Sons?" she managed.

I didn't blink.

"Yeah. Sons."

I let it sit there just long enough for it to finish counting—one, two, both—then opened my car door, slid into the seat, and tossed my last line like a lit match:

"Have a nice day."

Then I drove away.

No dramatic music.
No slow-motion walk.

Just me, leaving her in the smoke of her own assumptions.

Was it petty? Absolutely.
Was it healing? Not really.

I wasn't out there sleeping with everyone. I was using the only leverage I knew how to reach for in a world that had already taken too much from my body.

Call it oppositional defiance.

Call it self-destruction dressed up as power.

At the time, it felt like balance.

It was never about loving her sons.

It wasn't even about *them*.

It was about that girl at the kitchen table being told she was beneath them—and finally getting the chance to look the woman in charge in the eye and say, without stuttering:

You were wrong about me.

You were wrong about them.

And you don't get to define my worth.

That was my first real taste of getting back.

Here's what it taught my body: power can feel like heat and still not feel like safety.

It wasn't pretty.

It wasn't clean.

Just a girl who'd been underestimated her whole life, deciding that people were going to call her a problem—

She might as well be the kind they remember.

CHAPTER TWO

Too Good for My Chaos

***

$\mathcal{L}$ater that summer, I was nineteen—and already exhausted in a way that had nothing to do with age.

I wasn't healed. I wasn't growing. I wasn't "on a journey."
I was just surviving. One foot in front of the other. One day at a time. Breathing because my body hadn't figured out how to quit yet.

Revenge had woken something up in me. But it didn't give me any peace. I was still mad at everything what I'd lived through, what I'd lost, the people who'd walked away, the people who stayed in all the wrong ways. I felt like I was always three seconds from snapping or shutting down.

So, I did what a lot of kids with too much going on up there.

I went where the noise was louder than my head.

There was this teen dance club, dark and sweaty and loud, where the music was so heavy you could feel it in your chest. It was a place you went when you didn't have much money but needed to feel like you existed outside your own thoughts for a few hours.

That's where I ran into him.

He was there with his friends, posted up like they owned the place, but not in that aggressive way. More like they were holding each other up just by being there together.

He was funny. Not "trying too hard" funny. Just quick, real, someone that slid under your defenses before you could block it. His personality had this light to it

Like he was carrying around his own little sun and letting people stand in it for a minute.

Every time he was around, the darkness in my head backed up a step.
Not gone. Just... quieter.

We started talking more. Seeing each other at the club. Texting. Laughing. That slow, hopeful thing started to happen where you remember what it's like to be *liked*, not just used.

He lived with his mom in a low-income apartment complex. His friends lived there too. The place people love to judge from the outside without ever stepping foot in the parking lot.

But that parking lot was its own world.

They would all hang out there at night, leaning on cars, sitting on hoods, talking about everything and nothing. Planning futures. Making promises to themselves out loud: how they were going to get out, get more, break the chain of what they'd grown up in.

It wasn't empty talk, either. You could hear it in their voices. They wanted more.

I watched him with them and something in me softened.

He respected his mom. I mean "really" respected her. He never brought girls inside. He didn't sneak anyone in. It wasn't because he couldn't, but because he cared what she thought and cared about her house.

He had all this heart, all this potential, this drive to be better than what he'd been handed.

And then there was me

Still angry, still raw, still walking around with revenge in my teeth like a habit I couldn't kick.

We started dating if you could call it that. It was soft around the edges. Not official, not defined. But he made me feel like a person and that alone scared me more than anything.

When you've been treated like trash long enough, kindness feels suspicious.

Being seen feels dangerous.

One night, he decided to risk it.

He snuck me into his room.

It felt like the biggest rebellion in the world, even though all we were really doing was trying to exist in the same space without the rest of the world barging in.

The problem was his mom.

He couldn't have girls over. That was the rule. And unlike most guys his age, he actually respected it. But that night, he wanted me there anyway. Wanted to be close. Wanted to take me out of whatever storm I was walking under, even if it was just for a few hours.

So we made a plan

He slid me under his bed.

Literally.

I spent the whole night under there, pressed against the floorboards, dust in my nose, heart racing every time the building creaked.

He didn't just leave me there and crawl up on top of the mattress. He climbed under the bed with me. Curled around me in that tiny space, arms around me, like his body could build a wall between me and everything else.

No sex. No pressure. Just him holding me in the dark.

I don't think he realized how strange that felt to me, to be that close to someone and not have them want to take something. To have someone just *be there* without treating my body like a debt they were collecting on.

Something I have never felt, safe.

Not forever. Not fully. Just for that night. Under that bed.

Morning came anyway.

You can hold your breath for a while, but reality always finds a way in.

We heard his mom start up the stairs.

That safety bubble popped fast.

We locked eyes under the bed, him wide-eyed, me already calculating how bad it could get, and he did what boys with too much imagination and not enough options do.

He whispered this great idea.

"Okay, listen. I'll open the window. You can climb out

and jump down onto the shed roof. Then slide off. She won't see you."

Second-story window. Shed roof. James Bond move with no training and no stunt double.

My fingers went numb on the window frame.

In my head, a part of me was thinking,

You've been through worse,

and another part went,

Of course this is how my morning is going

He opened the window. I squeezed out, heart pounding, trying not to fall face-first into the neighbor's life. I hit the roof of the shed, slid down, and dropped to the ground harder than I meant to.

Somewhere between the slide and the landing, the house shook just enough for his mom to notice.

She came into his room and said, "What was that?"

By then, I was already out of sight.

I don't know what he told her. I don't know how he explained the noise, or the open window, or why he was suddenly so awake. All I know is that I was gone, slipping away from the building, heart racing, shoes hitting the pavement.

And as I walked, something heavy hit me right between the ribs.

That was the day I realized he was too good for me.

Not because I was trash. Not because I was worthless. But because he still had dreams he believed in. And I was just trying to get through the week.

He and his friends would always stand in that parking lot at night, talking about breaking the chain, building a life, doing better. They were still young enough to picture a future and think they could reach it.

Me? I didn't have dreams. I had survival.

He had a mom he respected, a line he didn't want to cross, and a heart that still trusted people.

I had a storm inside me that didn't care who it hit.

I knew if I stayed in his life, I would drag my chaos into his plans. I would jeopardize every promise he'd made to himself in that parking lot. It wasn't I was trying to ruin anything, but because I didn't know how to exist without ruining things.

He wasn't ready for the kind of broken I was.

And I wasn't ready for his plans

Sometimes the most honest kind of love you can give someone is leaving before you turn into the hurricane that knocks down everything they're trying to build.

So I let him go.

Not with a big speech. Not with a dramatic ending.

Just with the quiet, painful understanding that some people are too good to be pulled into your storm, and that's if you care about them at all, you don't let them stay there.

The next one he'd be just broken enough to match my storm.

CHAPTER THREE

The Night I Fought Back

***

The same winter started it all. Over the next couple years, it escalated fast.

At nineteen, I was working, smiling on cue, and carrying my past like it was just another uniform.

I'd already lived through more than most grown adults talk about out loud. I didn't trust quiet, or "nice," or anything that looked too stable. I trusted my instincts, that's the only way I knew how to breathe.

When I met him at work, he made sense in the worst way.

It started simple with breaks at the same time, shared jokes over headsets, leaning just a little too close over cheap coffee. He noticed me. Not the case file version of me, not the "troubled past" version. Just me.

He told me I was strong. Told me I'd been through a lot. Said he admired how I kept going.

When you've spent your life being treated like a problem, admiration feels like a high

We started dating. I moved in with him. Then I married him.

I did what I'd always done: tried to become whatever somebody else needed.

He talked about wanting a better life, a way out, something more stable than bouncing between crap jobs. For him, the answer was a union job in a factory with steady pay, benefits, the thing people in our world bragged about getting.

While he was chasing that, I decided my way out would be different.

The military looked like structure and a path: housing, pay, a uniform that might erase where I came from. It looked like a place where rules meant something, where rank meant you'd earned your spot instead of just taking it.

So, I joined.

Basic training was hard, but fear wasn't new to me. I knew how to read faces, follow orders, and move fast when someone barked a command. I'd been trained for that long before I ever put on a uniform.

The uniform didn't erase my past. It just gave me a different set of people to survive.

One decided my body was his, whether I consented or not.

You can dress it up in any words you want. But it comes down to this:

I was violated by someone who outranked me, someone who was trained to lead.

The girl who once stood in a courtroom and told the truth didn't show up this time. The soldier did the one who understood what happens when you speak against someone with power.

I reported it.

I didn't get justice.

I got discharged and I didn't care.

They stamped my paperwork and sent me home like faulty equipment.

I flew back alone.

No husband waiting at the gate. No welcome-home sign. No "Are you okay?" Just announcements over the intercom and strangers dragging suitcases while I tried to remember which version of myself, I needed to be now.

I landed in Grand Rapids and called my husband.

He didn't come get me.

Gas was "too expensive." The drive was "too far." The excuses were cheap and easy.

So, I paid a ridiculous taxi fare to my best friend's house, sitting in the back seat, staring out the window, letting the message sink in: I'd survived the military, a disgusting violation. And a discharge... and still wasn't worth a tank of gas.

Later, he finally showed up at my friend's house. No flowers. No soft questions. Just a tired man who looked at me like my trauma was a bill he hadn't agreed to pay.

Not long after, a week to be exact, he decided he wanted a new car.

His credit was shot. Mine wasn't and I had a good job already

So, I signed for it. I put the loan in my name and the risk on my back, that's what "good" wives do in the stories we're told, carry the weight and hope it earns them safety.

He drove that car like it was a trophy.

He worked second shift at the factory.

Our lives bent around his schedule, his sleep, his meals, his moods. I fit myself into the cracks the way I always had with men who held the power to hurt me.

One night, I decided to do something nice.

We needed a win. I did a small gesture that could smooth the jagged edges of everything we weren't talking about. I grabbed fast food, got in my car, and drove to his job, imagining ten quiet minutes in the car together like we were just any other couple.

When I pulled into the lot, I spotted the car — the one in my name.

It was parked off to the side. Away from everyone else.

Windows steamed.

My brain tried to lie to me.

It's just cold out. It's the weather. Don't be dramatic. Don't make something out of nothing.

But my body knew. It always does.

I got out, bag of food in my hand, and walked closer.

I didn't need a full view. Movements. Shadows. Bare skin. That rhythm you recognize immediately

He was having sex with a coworker in the back seat of the car I was paying for.

The bag of fast food in my hand might as well have been a punchline.

I didn't bang on the window. I didn't scream. I didn't drag anyone out by their hair. I didn't give him a scene he could point to later and say, "See? She's crazy."

I turned around, went back to my car, and drove home.

Revenge is a language. That night, mine shifted from snarky to deadly fluent.

He usually got home around eleven p.m. I knew his schedule down to the minute. That night, I built my plan around it.

I went through the house and gathered his clothes, his shirts, his pants, his life scattered through the drawers like mold. I took them into the yard and made a pile.

I poured grill fluid all over them.

Then I lit it on fire.

Flames climbed the fabric. Smoke curled up into the dark, carrying the smell of burned cotton and all the pretending I was done doing.

For the first time, my anger took up real space.

Headlights swung into the driveway.

He hit the brakes when he saw the fire. Got out. Stared at the burning pile. Then at me.

I looked him dead in the eye and said, as calm as if I were commenting on the weather:

"I thought you might need extra light to make it to the porch."

That one sentence was everything I hadn't been allowed to be as a kid.

There, I swallowed everything.
Here, I was spitting fire.

For three solid seconds, I felt untouchable.

Then it shattered.

He rushed me, grabbed me, dragged me into the house.

The man who had promised "for better or for worse" moved like he'd finally picked "worse" and meant it.

He hit me. Over and over

This is the part of "standing up for yourself" that people don't like to talk about. They don't talk about how power hits back. How the moment you stop absorbing everything quietly, the violence can spike.

And then he escalated.

He stabbed me. Twice in my shoulder

The first stab was shock — white and blinding. The second was clarity: ***He really wants me to break***

Pain spread hot, then distant. I fell into the corner of the living room while he kept kicking, his boot slamming into my hip until the bone chipped.

His dad was asleep down the hall and never came out once.

Blood. Heat. A high-pitched ringing in my ears. Two stab wounds. A chipped hip. My body doing what it had always done in danger — trying to shut down enough to stay alive.

The room started to blur and tilt. My edges went gray.

Through the haze, I looked at him and forced out: "Don't fall asleep."

It was part threat, part promise, part animal instinct. If I lived, this wouldn't be the end.

Then everything went dark.

When I woke up, it was quiet.

The clock said 2 a.m.

My body felt like shattered glass. Standing wasn't an option. So I did the only thing I could.

I crawled.

Elbows, forearms, fingers digging into the floor. An army crawl across my own living room, leaving a thin line of blood behind me like proof I'd been there.

I made it to the kitchen.

My hand closed around the handle of a frying pan — heavy, solid, familiar. A cooking tool that, in that moment, became the only weapon I had.

I dragged myself down the hallway to the bedroom where we had a waterbed, that ridiculous "adult comfort" floating in the middle of our disaster.

I braced myself on the edge, pulled my broken body up, and used what strength I had left to launch myself at him.

I swung.

The pan connected with his face with a wet, solid crack. He jerked awake, gargling, eyes wild, disoriented. The hit cut straight through whatever fog he was in.

I wasn't the only one getting hurt.
I was drawing the line.

I staggered out to the front porch, blood drying down the left side of my shirt, hands shaking so hard I could barely hold the phone.

I dialed 911.

"My name is Paige," I said. *"I think I killed my husband."*

There's no script for those words. No guidebook for that kind of night. Just a dispatcher on the other end trying to keep you talking while the life you built burns down behind you.

The sirens came. Red and blue lights painted the house. Neighbors peeked from behind curtains, watching a story they'd never guessed was happening next door.

They loaded us into separate ambulances. He gargled and moaned, face swollen and broken. I lay there, hip screaming, wounds throbbing, mind strangely calm in the middle of the wreck.

At the hospital, a cop stood between our beds and asked him if he wanted to press charges against me.

I was right there when he answered.

"No," he said. *"I want a divorce."*

That was it. Not an apology. Not a denial. Just an exit.

People like to imagine this is the part where everything gets better — where someone steps in, sees what happened, and wraps you in safety.

That's not what happened.

When the adrenaline faded and the questions started — police, hospital staff, forms, And when they asked who they should call, I didn't answer right away.

Hospital air has its own smell — bleach, plastic, and something metallic that sticks to the back of your throat. My skin felt too tight, like my body didn't know where to put the shock. Nurses talked in calm voices that didn't match the scene in my head. Forms slid onto clipboards. Questions landed like stones.

And I kept thinking: if I say the wrong thing, they'll decide I'm the problem.

That fear is its own kind of hand around your throat. It doesn't leave bruises. But it keeps you quiet.

I didn't have anyone to save me.

No soft place to land. No "come stay with me." No one who knew the whole story and chose me anyway.

Everyone I could think of either didn't know, wouldn't believe, or would use it against me.

There was only one number that ever answered when things turned violent.

My dad.

The same man who molested me.

The same man whose house taught me how to leave my body and watch bad things happen from somewhere far away.

This was his territory: fists, knives, cops, and big messes.

I knew if I opened that door back to him, everything the courts had tried to build — new name, new start,

distance — would crack. All the boundaries I'd fought to hold would go soft.

But lying there, bleeding, afraid they were going to decide I was the monster in this story; I didn't see another option.

Reaching for that phone felt like choosing between two kinds of danger.

On one side was a system I didn't trust.
On the other side was the man who had already destroyed my childhood. .
I called him anyway.
Because when your whole life has been built inside violence, sometimes the only person you know to ask for help is the same person who taught you what fear is in the first place.
Here's what that taught my body: Fear reaches for what it knows.
That was the night fighting back saved my life—
—and the night I pulled my past right back into it.

CHAPTER FOUR

Borrowed Safety

***

As winter broke into spring, I left town on borrowed safety.

When I called my dad from that hospital bed

He didn't show up himself. He never did, not when there was a way to keep his hands clean. Instead, he "handled it."

He arranged for one of his "friends" to pick me up and get me out of state for a while. As if I was evidence that needed to be moved, not a daughter who needed to be safe.

The friend showed up, loaded me and what little I had into a vehicle, and drove me across the state line to a house that didn't look anything like the places I came from.

The house was big and beautiful.

Mirrored tint on the windows so you could look out without anyone looking in. A pond in the backyard that looked like someone had ordered it from a catalog. A sauna. A jacuzzi tub room lined in cedar like a spa. Everything smelled like money and wood polish instead of cigarettes and fear.

Next door was their factory — huge, metal, loud when it ran, a building that said: we make things here. And we make a lot of them.

Susan, the friend's mom took me in.

She didn't treat me like a burden. She didn't talk to me like a favor she had to do because of some debt owed to my dad. She treated me like a daughter she never got to have.

She cooked for me. Checked on me. Asked how I slept. Bought me things I never would have asked for. Made space for me in her home like it was the most natural thing in the world.

I finally could breathe.

But when you've been locked up emotionally your whole life, that first breath doesn't always come out gentle. It explodes.

I was like a dog that had been locked in a cage too long. As soon as the gate opened, I didn't walk out slowly and sit in the grass.

I went crazy.

I started bar hopping with a girl I clicked with right away. We'd get ready together, laughing too loud, spraying on cheap body spray like armor. We hit bars and dance clubs I never knew existed — dark, loud, pulsing with music that drowned out the noise in my own head.

We danced until my feet hurt. Until my lungs burned. Until my thoughts blurred out into beat and sweat and neon.

Men were everywhere.

Susan, was always keeping an eye out, like the world was a buffet and I needed to pick something decent.

"This one has a good job"
"This one's really sweet"
"He's got his head on straight. You should give him a
chance."

She tried to set me up more than once.

But nothing stuck. They all felt like static. Faces, names, phone numbers handed to me like business cards I didn't plan to keep. For a while, nothing cut deep enough to feel real.

Then the pattern shifted — but not in the way it used to.

It wasn't "fall in love fast, move in, call it a future." This time it was smaller, quieter. Just something to do. Someone to occupy my time so I didn't have to sit alone with the storm in my head.

Meanwhile, I stayed down there for about a year.

I got a job at a distribution company. Clocked in, clocked out. Went home to a nice house that didn't belong to me and a woman who treated me like I mattered. Went out at night and pretended that meant I was "enjoying life."

In a way, I was.

Compared to where I'd been, it felt like a vacation — a soft landing on borrowed safety. But divorce doesn't evaporate just because you cross a state line.

Eventually, the papers caught up.

Divorce court came.

I had to face him one last time.

Or at least, I thought.

I drove back for court, my stomach knotted. Susan wasn't about to allow me to walk in there looking weak.

She took me shopping and pulled a knockout outfit off the rack—something that fit me just right, that made me stand a little taller when I looked in the mirror.

"You want him to really regret his choices," she said.

She wasn't wrong.

I walked into that courthouse looking like every "you'll never make it" they'd ever thrown at me had just bounced off. We went through the motions — questions, signatures, legal words that boiled down to: this is done.

By the time we walked outside, the story should have been over.

I should have gotten in my car, driven back to that big house, and started the next chapter of my life.

Instead, I ended the day exactly where I shouldn't have:

In his bed.

Stupid me.

What was I thinking?

The truth is, it didn't take much.

He knew which strings to pull — familiarity, guilt, promises. All the classics.

It'll be better this time.

I've changed.

We needed a reset.

Now that this is behind us, we can start over.

And some part of me, the part that still believed broken things could somehow rearrange themselves into a fairytale, listened

We went and found a place to rent.

No more living in his dad's house.

Now we had a little place of our own, about two miles down the road from his dad. Close enough for his family to still circle, close enough that nothing was really new—just repackaged.

On paper, it looked like progress: married again, new house, fresh start.

Underneath, it was the same old story with a different mailing address.

That same week, the fair came to town.

I went because that's what you do when life doesn't make sense and a fair shows up like a temporary universe — lights, smells, rides that spin you fast enough to blur everything.

That's where I saw him.

Jeff

In high school, he had been my best friend. Back then, he was this scrawny little boy who talked 500 miles an hour. Annoying as hell sometimes, but in a way that distracted the storm in my head. He was noise that didn't hurt.

Now, he wasn't a boy at all.

He was tall. Filled out. Handsome. A man you notice right away, of course he got my attention as I got his.

We recognized each other instantly.

He fell into step beside me and we walked the whole fair together — from the food stands to the midway, past the rides and lights and crowds. It felt weirdly easy, like no time had passed and a lifetime had passed at the same time.

For a few hours, I let myself exist in that pocket — just me and Jeff, with no courtrooms, no bruises, no frying pans, no dads, no ex-husbands.

Then the fair night ended. And I went back to the place I was calling home.

I walked in the door and, for once, I was excited to share something.

"I ran into Jeff at the fair," I told my ex. *"You remember him?"*

I didn't get to say anything more.

He grabbed me.

His hands clamped down on my arms so hard they left bruises almost instantly. He threw me around, his anger slamming into me before I even understood what had triggered it.

Jealousy. Control. Insecurity. It didn't matter what we named it. It landed the same way: violence.

I cried out with a destructive scream that came from somewhere way deeper than that moment. It wasn't him grabbing me. It was about every time someone had laid hands on me and called it love.

My legs gave out. I dropped to my knees.

He left for work like nothing had happened.

That was his pattern: break something, walk out the door, punch a timecard.

As soon as he was gone, I grabbed my keys, got in my car, and drove.

I drove to where Jeff was staying.

When Jeff opened the door and saw me, the first thing he noticed were the bruises on my arms.

His face changed.

The easy, funny guy from the fair vanished. In his place was someone hard and steady.

He demanded to know what happened. I didn't have to go into detail; the marks did most of the talking. He told me he was going to take care of it.

I panicked.

Because as much as I hated being hurt, I was terrified of being homeless again. I still hadn't found a job since the move back. I didn't have an income. A backup plan, and not a safety net except the same man who kept hurting me.

In my head, the equation was still twisted:
Violence + roof = survival.
No violence = no roof = no survival.

So when Jeff said he'd handle it, fear shot through me right alongside the relief.

He waited until the weekend.

Then he showed up at the house.

He walked in like he belonged there, like he'd made up his mind and nothing was going to move it. He went straight to my ex and didn't waste time with speeches.

He grabbed him. Threw him right out the door — him and his stuff. Clothes, whatever he could push out with him.

"You will never touch her again," Jeff said.

Just like that.

The line was drawn.

I started screaming.

Not at Jeff—but at everything. At the fear. At the cliff I suddenly realized I was standing on.

"What am I going to do?" I yelled. *"What am I going to do now?"*

The room spun with that weird silence after a fight—the kind where you can hear your own heartbeat and suddenly notice the air is cold because the door has been open too long.

I had nothing. Just a house and a history of everything falling apart.

Jeff looked at me, steady and sure, and said the words I'd always wanted to hear and never knew how to hold:

"I've always loved you. I will take care of you."

That should have been the moment everything finally turned into a love story.

But my life doesn't do neat chapters and clean turns.

It does borrowed safety. Rescues with strings I can't see yet. Men who mean well stepping into a storm they don't fully understand.

Still, in that moment — standing in the doorway of a house that had just spit out one abuser and pulled in a man who claimed he loved me—

I decided to believe him.

What else did I have

And because part of me still thought that being chosen, being "taken care of," might finally fix my way of being broken that had been growing in me since before I even had words for it.

CHAPTER FIVE

All Gas, No Brakes

***

The divorce was final. By early fall, Jeff was there.

If my life had a theme song during this time, it would've just been one long electric guitar solo: loud, chaotic, and absolutely not safe for quiet neighborhoods.

Back then, our world was late-night drives, loud love, and a little home that never stayed quiet for long.

When Jeff threw my ex out and told me he loved me, it was like somebody slammed a big red RESET button. Suddenly, instead of dodging fists and lies, I was with my best friend from high school. And we were stupid in love.

It was like the universe finally handed me a co-pilot who could keep up with my crazy.

We laughed constantly.
We touched constantly.
We breathed, but mostly just between rounds.

We didn't miss a beat with each other. There was no awkward warm-up, no "getting to know you" stage. We went straight from zero to "this is my person" with the speed of a car you probably shouldn't drive on a dirt road.

Was it healthy? Probably not.
Was it amazing? Absolutely.

For once, my life felt less like survival and more like a ride I actually wanted to be on.

Then we decided we wanted a baby.

Not "one day." Not "once we're more stable."

Nope.

NOW.

There is "trying to have a baby," and then there is whatever we were doing.

We were on a mission.

Every time we looked at each other: "Baby practice."

Every time we left the house: "Public baby practice."

If there was a horizontal surface, we considered it a sign.

Cars.

Woods.

Parking lots.

Parks.

Parties.

If that area had a nickname, we probably added an asterisk to it.

We found this little pond out in the woods that became our unofficial headquarters. It was quiet, surrounded by trees, and just secluded enough to make bad ideas feel extra brilliant.

One night we were out there being **extremely** enthusiastic about our baby project when we learned we were not, in fact, alone.

Hidden out in the dark were hunters, already set up and waiting for first light.

Instead of deer, they got us.

Right in the middle of things, we heard this voice yell from the tree line:

"GET HER!"

Like they were the world's most inappropriate hype squad.

I should've been mortified. Instead, I almost died laughing.

That was us in a nutshell: loud, ridiculous, and way too into each other to care who was watching from the shadows.

Every new month turned into the same ritual.

Hope.

Test.

Wait.

Negative.

Again.

And again.

I'd stare at those little sticks like they were personally insulting me.

"Oh, you don't see two lines? Say it to my face."

It started to feel like the universe was messing with us on purpose.

Then one day, after a whole stack of "nope," it finally happened.

Two lines.

Just like that: pregnant.

It felt unreal.All those half-joked "this is the one" moments, the thing we'd been trying to create on purpose was actually happening

We were going to have a baby.

For once, my body didn't betray me.

The pregnancy went smoothly. Just steady appointments, kicks that felt like tiny drum solos, and me alternating between:

"I've got this,"

and

"Who trusted me with a whole human?"

We decided on a private birthing center instead of a regular hospital. Something calmer. Softer. More personal. Like if we planned the setting right, the story would go exactly how we pictured it.

That was adorable of us.

By the time I went into labor, Jeff had lost his driver's license. Because of course he had.

So there I am, in full-blown labor, and guess who's behind the wheel?

The man with no license.

Every bump in the road felt like my uterus was trying to exit the chat. Every imaginary siren in my head was a cop ready to pull us over and ask why this idiot was driving while his very pregnant, very screaming girlfriend was in the passenger seat.

The whole way, I'm yelling:

"You can't DRIVE! You are literally NOT ALLOWED TO DRIVE!"

"I'm going to have this baby in the back of a cop car!"
"They're going to arrest you and I'm going to crown in county orange!"

Jeff just kept saying, *"It's fine, it's fine,"* like that was a valid medical plan.

I finally reached my limit and told him to pull into the local hospital before I gave birth on the dashboard out of spite.

We screeched into the parking lot. And I looked at him and said,

"That's it. You're done. Call someone with an actual license."

So he did.

He called his grandma.

And bless that woman — she showed up like the cavalry. Calm, collected, fully licensed.

She drove us the rest of the way to the birthing center, like,

"Oh, is someone having a baby and someone else being dumb?"

Because of that detour, she got to be there when her great-grandson was born.

After all that — no license, my screaming, the hospital pit stop because my anxiety had a valid point — we ended up exactly where we'd planned:

Private birthing center.
Me in labor.

Jeff with his "I'm trying" face.
His grandma sitting there like the backbone of the whole operation.

Then there he was.

Levi

Loud. Alive.

Brand-new to a world that had already tried to wipe his parents off the map more than once.

For a minute, everything slowed down. It was just us. Me, Jeff, his grandma, and this tiny human who had no idea the circus he'd just been born into.

The next day, less than twenty-four hours after I pushed a whole person into existence, we packed Levi up and headed home.

This is where other people tell stories about soft blankets and calm rides and "I watched him sleep the whole way and cried."

Not me.

On the way home, we realized the dog was out of food.

Of course he was.

Because why wouldn't my first day as a mom come with a side quest?

We pulled into the feed store.

I got out of the car like I hadn't just had a baby yesterday. slow walk didn't exist, and who had time to take it easy. Just full "I'm fine" performance mode.

I walked in, found the biggest bag of dog food like I was actively trying to piss off my pelvic floor, and heaved it up onto my shoulder.

The cashier looked at me like,

"Ma'am... are you sure?"

I looked back like,

"I've made worse decisions."

I stood there in line, holding that bag, while my body quietly filed HR complaints.

Then I walked back out to the car with it still on my shoulder, where Jeff and tiny, brand-new Levi were waiting.

No announcement. or "Look what I did!"
Just a silent, aggressive conversation between me and the universe:

Having a kid is not going to break me.
I can still carry heavy things.
I can still handle it

On the outside, it probably looked ridiculous:

Freshly postpartum woman hauling a giant bag of dog food like she was training for the World's Strongest Mom competition.

On the inside?

I was tired. I was sore. I was bleeding.
But I was also stubborn as hell.

If motherhood was going to test me, I was determined to fail the "fragile" section and ace the "feral" one.

If my life had a welcome mat for this chapter, it would've said:

Just gave birth. Still lifting feed bags. Sleep later.

I didn't know it yet, but Levi wasn't just going to be my baby.

He was about to be the mirror that showed me every
crack I'd been hiding.

But for a little while, it was just this:

Me.

 Jeff

A brand-new baby.

And a feed store parking lot where I decided — even if
my whole life was crazy — I was going to carry it
myself.

CHAPTER SIX

Wheels Came Off (and Rolled Back Around)

***

The year of diapers, bills, and love getting heavy.

Somewhere between midnight bottles and morning feed runs, I started noticing it: Jeff was dying a little.

Not in the dramatic, movie kind of dying. The quiet kind.

Not dropping dead in the kitchen. Just... dimming.

It wasn't one big moment. It was a collection of small ones. The way he stared past the room like he was already somewhere else. The way his laugh came a half-second late. The way his shoulders sagged after work — not from tired, but from something heavier. And I felt it in my own chest like a slow leak: this isn't the same love story anymore.
It was still love. It just wasn't light.

The guy who used to match my energy shot for shot — the one who thought having sex in the woods while hunters yelled "Get her!" was peak romance — that spark started to fade.

It wasn't that he didn't love Levi. He did. He held him, changed diapers, did the dad stuff. But every once in a while, when the house went quiet, I'd catch a look on his face that said:

I miss the old us.

The pond.
The late-night drives.
The freedom to be idiots without a car seat in the back.

I missed us too.

So, I did the "mature" thing you're not really supposed to say out loud.

I sat him down.

"You don't have to stay," I told him. *"If you want to go enjoy your life, I'm not going to blame you."*

Part of me meant it. Part of me wanted him to fight for us. To say, ***I'm here. I chose this. I chose you***

He stayed.

For a while.

But you can only live a life your heart isn't in for so long before something cracks.

By the time Levi was around nine months old, I was working in a factory.

Not a Pinterest craft factory. A loud, metal, OSHA-nightmare kind of factory.

We produced huge metal filing cabinets that came down toward us on a rack overhead, like heavy, rectangular wrecking balls in single file. Our job was to pull them off as they rolled by.

Now add this detail: I'm short.

So there I am, under a moving line of giant metal boxes designed for taller people and built to hold the weight of other people's problems.

You can probably feel the disaster creeping in.

One day, a guy didn't see me.

He grabbed a cabinet off the rack. It slipped.

Cabinet.

Gravity.

My head.

I didn't have a dramatic ducking or reflexes. Just impact.

I ended up with a concussion bad enough that my brain swelled.

Suddenly, It wasn't only "tired, traumatized mom." I was "traumatic brain injury" mom.

I had to see specialists — actual professionals — whose job was to teach me how to walk and talk again.

Walking.

Talking.

Things I'd been doing since before I knew my times tables.

My memory got scrambled. My words came out wrong. My body moved like my brain was lagging behind real life.

They clapped when I walked straight. I wanted to scream.

I tried to joke about it:

"Limited edition: childhood trauma AND brain damage. Collect them all."

But underneath the jokes, I was scared.

And Jeff?

He was scared too. Just in a different direction.

He had a young child. An ex — wild-child girlfriend who now moved and spoke like somebody had unplugged her halfway through her download.

This wasn't what he'd pictured when he'd thrown my ex out and said, *"I'll take care of you."*

Here's where the truth stings:

He didn't stay in it with me.

I had to move in with a woman who could take care of me and Levi while I tried to learn how to be a functioning human again. She fed us, housed us, helped me through the basic rehab that makes you realize how fragile everything is.

Somewhere in that mess, while I was relearning how to walk and string sentences together,

Jeff decided to walk away.

He didn't make a big announcement with a speech. He just... shifted out of my life. Less boyfriend. More "baby's dad who stops by."

I got better enough over time to get my own apartment — me and Levi, just us. Single mom with a rattled brain and a kid on her hip.

Jeff would still come around.

But not as my partner anymore.

Just as Levi's dad.

He'd visit, play with Levi, catch up, then slip little pieces of his new life into the conversation.

That's when I started hearing about her.

The girl from work.

He didn't say it viciously. It wasn't, "Look at my new upgrade." It was more like:

"I'm talking to this girl at work..."

And I sat there listening, understanding more than he realized.

I should've learned right there what kind of man he'd be in the future.

The kind who finds a new woman while the old one is learning to walk straight again. The kind who can emotionally move on while you're still fighting with your own brain just to function.

But then, all I thought was:

How can I blame him for not wanting to be tied to my incompetency?

It was easier to beat myself up than admit that he'd already made his choice.

Then slowly, quietly, stubbornly—

I started getting better.

My words came back cleaner. My balance improved. My memory stopped dropping important pieces of my life like breadcrumbs.

The fog didn't evaporate overnight, but one day I realized:

I was back.

Not fully healed or shiny and new. But me.

The spunky, wild, nothing-keeps-me-down version of me that had gone missing. The one who lit clothes on fire in the yard. The one who swung frying pans at the right heads. The one who did not go quietly.

And once she was back, the whole "he's got a girl at work" thing hit different.

Because now it wasn't:

"He left a broken girl."

It was:

"He left me. And I am not broken anymore."

I snapped.

Not the blackout rage kind of snap.

A controlled one.

The kind where you know exactly what you're capable of and exactly how far you're choosing not to go... yet.

I showed up at his job.

He was inside living his new little life. And I was in the parking lot staring at his car like it had personally insulted me.

I was fully ready, in my head, to break every window out of that thing.

Not a cute "oops, cracked your windshield" moment. I'm talking full-on automotive biblical plague.

My hands were shaking so hard I felt it in my teeth. My throat tasted like metal.

My feet were planted like if I moved, I'd turn into the version of me everyone expects.

I saw it: each swing, each crash, the way the whole place would go quiet

But here's the plot twist:
I didn't do it.

I stood on the edge of that line and realized something wild:

I had control.

Real control.

Not the pretend kind I used to fake while my life was actually running me ragged. I felt all that old heat, all that anger, all that righteous fury—

and I could choose where it went.

So instead of taking it out on his windows, I made sure he saw me.

The real me.

Not the stumbling, healing version. Not the half-there girl he walked away from. The full-force, talk-back, don't-you-dare-count-me-out version.

And she was not subtle.

That other girl?

She got the picture.

You can't really compete with the ex who almost died, came back swinging, and is now standing in your man's work parking lot radiating "I will rebuild my entire life and you will *watch*" energy.

He followed me back to my apartment.

That alone told me he wasn't as "over it" as he'd been pretending.

He walked in and looked at me — not past me, not around me, not through me.

At me. And I saw it land: I was back.

Not the broken mother of his child.

Not the girl he stopped loving out of fear and fatigue.

The spunky, wild person I used to be. The one that nothing could really keep down for long. The one who, no matter what got thrown at her — fists, courts, cabinets from the ceiling — kept getting back up.

And that's when he did it.

He proposed.

It wasn't fairy lights. No kneeling in rose petals. No "will you marry me?" scripted for Instagram.

Just this man who had left me when I was at my worst, standing there in my apartment, realizing I was still the best thing he was ever going to get—

asking me to make it official.

If this were a different story, this might be the part where I say:

And we lived happily ever after

But this is my story.

The proposal wasn't the end of "ever after."

It was proof I still hadn't learned my lesson about the kind of man he was.

It was the start of a brand-new round.

CHAPTER SEVEN

Inviting the Wolf to the Wedding

***

*T*wo summers later, we got married.

By the time wedding talk started floating around, my gut was already whispering that we were making a deal with a storm.

For a minute, our little circus felt steady again.

It wasn't peaceful with a white picket fence, but it was my place.

Wild, crazy, fun chaotic — with a child.

Me, Jeff, and Levi were like our own little circus act. Sleep was optional. Adventures were not. We had bills, sure, and responsibilities, but there was still that spark. The stupid laughter. The bad ideas. The feeling that no matter how sideways things went, we'd figure it out.

For a minute, I almost believed this was it.
My story had finally settled into something good.

Then it happened.

My dad came back.

He came back older. Calmer on the surface. Wiser in that way men get when they've outlived enough of their own bad choices to talk about them like lessons instead of crimes.

He didn't sneak in. He called. He showed up. He stood there, this aging version of the man who had wrecked my childhood, and acted like he wanted to make things right.

The difference this time was that I wasn't a kid.

I had a son.

And I had Jeff

Jeff knew about my past. I had finally told him what my dad had done, what that house had been, what "family" had meant for me. Saying it out loud had felt like peeling my own skin back.

So when my dad reappeared, I wasn't as worried as I should've been.

Because in my head, the math looked like this:

Trauma + grown woman + protective partner + baby =

He can't hurt me like that again.

I had a buffer now. A shield. A man next to me who I thought would throw himself between me and anything that ever tried to break me again.

So I did something I'd sworn I'd never do.

I listened.

Jeff was the one who really surprised me.

He didn't just tolerate my dad hovering at the edges.

He liked him.

To Jeff, my dad wasn't "the guy who broke the girl I love."

He was an asset.

My dad knew motors, engines, and machines. All the stuff Jeff's eyes lit up over. To him, Ray wasn't an abuser with a past — it was a walking encyclopedia of horsepower and torque with free hands-on training attached.

"I know what he did," Jeff told me. "But people change. You've got to forgive at some point. I won't let him hurt you again."

He said it like a promise and a plan.

Forgive him.

Use his knowledge.

Keep you safe.

He framed it like healing.

What I didn't see yet was how much he expected me to swallow and be silent.

I should have heard the alarm bells.

Instead, I heard this:

If Jeff wasn't scared of my dad, I didn't have to be either.

And my dad?

He leaned right into the role.

He played older, wiser, softer. He told stories about the past with just enough regret baked in to sound like he'd done reflection work, but not enough to actually take responsibility.

We didn't sit down and say the words:

"I forgive you for molesting me."

There was no formal ceremony.

It was more like... slowly backing away from the truth until everyone could call it "the past" and not choke on it.

Jeff kept nudging that door open.

"You deserve a dad," he'd say.

"He's trying."

"We'll make sure he can't cross any lines again."

He sounded so sure. Like having him there meant the danger was automatically contained.

And I wanted so badly to believe that.

Because the idea of having a normal moment with family picture, or a normal anything with the man who'd destroyed so much of me?

That was a kind of bait I didn't even know I was still hungry for.

So, when wedding talks started. And we were piecing together what that day would look like, the unthinkable slid onto the table like it was reasonable:

My dad walking me down the aisle.

You know how people get misty talking about that moment?

"The first man who ever loved me escorting me to the one who will love me forever."

Yeah. No.

The first man who ever hurt me escorting me to the man I believed would never let that happen again.

That was my version.

I didn't forget.

Let me repeat that: I did not forget.

I didn't suddenly rewrite my childhood into some Hallmark special where my dad was strict but loving. The memories didn't change. The courtrooms didn't vanish. The new name didn't undo what the old one had lived through.

What changed was my calculation of risk.

I eased my guard down.

Because I had Jeff

I convinced myself it was safe.

My dad would only ever be around me with Jeff there, watching. He wouldn't get me alone. He wouldn't have that same kind of power. I wasn't a frightened girl anymore.

I was a grown woman, a mother, engaged to a man who knew the truth and promised to protect me.

So, on that day, in that dress, with all those eyes on me—

I let my father put his hand on my arm and walk me toward the man at the altar.

The same man who had molested me as a child. The same man the courts had once tried to protect me from.

You know how photographers try to capture "the moment" a bride walks toward her future?

If you looked at that picture, you'd probably see what everyone else saw:

A father.

A daughter.

A wedding.

What you wouldn't see was the tightness in my chest telling myself over and over:

It's fine. Jeff is here. He won't let anything happen. This is normal. This is what normal people do.

My dad walked me down the aisle.

And somewhere under all the white fabric and flowers and fake peace, the younger version of me — the one who knew better — was screaming:

You just put the wolf in the family photos

From the outside, it looked like forgiveness.

From the inside, it was something else entirely:

A woman who had survived hell, trying so hard to have a "normal" life that she invited the devil to her wedding and called it healing.

CHAPTER EIGHT

The Cost of Being Useful

***

The winter after our wedding, being useful started costing more than I could pay.

When my dad first came back, he didn't show up as the monster from my childhood.

Years later, he drifted back into my life like he hadn't earned the right to know where I lived, like my door was still his to knock on.

He slipped back into the role he'd always liked best: Superhero Dad.

The storyteller.

The protector.

The man with the wild adventure memories.

He'd go on about "the old days" like they were golden: the trips we took when I was a kid, the things we did, the shit he framed as fun instead of trauma. If you only heard his version, you'd think I'd grown up in some off-brand Disney movie, less singing animals, more "edge."

And part of me wanted to believe him.

Part of me missed that dad. The one my brain had edited into the highlight reel so I could survive the rest.

Then he leveled up the act.

He offered me a job.

It not just any job.

It was with his attorney friend, working on a case about protecting kids from the system.

If there was ever a way to hook me clean through the heart, that was it.

Protecting kids?

Making sure the system didn't screw them over the way it did me?

I was in before he finished the sentence.

My dad knew exactly what he was doing.

Suddenly, I was traveling. Not just down the road, but flying in private planes, visiting different parts of the country. Me. The girl who'd been shoved around by the system now knocking on doors, tracking down kids who were adults now and had their own stories of what the state did or didn't do.

We weren't just telling sad stories.

We were fighting.

We pushed cases aimed at changing how Michigan handled removals. How easy it was to rip kids out of homes. What counted as "unfit."

No more taking kids just because there were dirty dishes in the sink.

No more pulling them because a grandparent thought they could "do better" and wanted to play hero.

Bit by bit, it stripped some of the god-complex power out of protective services. Forced people to stop treating kids like property they could just reassign when they didn't like how a family looked from the outside.

More kids started going home.

Not to perfection. To parents who were actually being given a chance to work on whatever the complaints were instead of just getting their children terminated like a bad lease.

And when it was real abuse?

When it was physical harm and real danger?

That's where the laws got harder.

Less, "Well, maybe," and more, "You don't get another chance to break this kid."

It also became easier for kids to go to relatives instead of strangers — less "cash cow for the state," more actual family.

I was helping build that.

I was in rooms that mattered. On flights that weren't just escape routes. On the receiving end of people actually listening when I talked.

For the first time, I felt important.

Heard.

All the shit I'd lived through had a purpose.

Then the attorney got weak.

He got wrapped up with one of his clients.

Not professionally.

Personally.

You don't have to be a lawyer to know that's the fast lane to "you're screwed."

He was looking at large penalties from the Bar Association. Reputation damaged. The thing that could take everything we'd built — the cases, the arguments, the law changes — and set it all on fire.

That's when my dad got a "great idea."

If you're hearing ominous music in your head right now, you're correct.

To him, there was a "simple" solution.

It was time for me to take one for the team.

Again.

You're waiting for the catch, aren't you?

He called me like it was just another strategy meeting.

He said *"I needed to claim that I was in a relationship with the attorney."*

Not the client. Me.

Oh, and one more thing?

I needed to say *"I was pregnant with his baby."*

At that time, Jeff and I were actually pregnant with our second child.

But in my dad's head, that was just an inconvenience. A scheduling conflict. A detail to rearrange.

"You need to make a statement that you and the attorney are together and that's his kid," he said *"And make it believable."*

He didn't ask.

He instructed.

When I pushed back, all the old version of him came flooding out, the weaponized, sharpened, aimed right at my life.

He didn't talk about the work, the kids, the laws, the purpose.

He talked about destruction.

"If you don't do it, I'm moving forward and telling Jeff," he said. *"And then you won't be able to repair it. I'll make sure of it."*

There it was.

The same man who had destroyed my childhood, now threatening to destroy the only real happiness I'd built as an adult:

My family.

I pleaded.

I told him this would wreck my marriage. That Jeff was the only real stability I'd ever had. That two year old Levi and this new baby growing inside me deserved better than watching their parents blown apart by some legal cover-up they didn't ask for.

I told him it would destroy Jeff

He did not care.

To him, this was a chess move.

I was a piece.

Sacrifice one to save the board.

He spun it like duty. Like the work we were doing was too important to let one man's stupidity ruin it.

I had to sacrifice in order for these changes to protect kids to go into effect.

That was the story he gave me. Like I was Joan of Arc with a stack of legal briefs.

In reality?

It was the same old pattern:

His mess.

His choices.

His threats.

My life on the line.

And once again, I broke myself trying to protect other people.

I told Jeff

It wrecked him.

There's no pretty way to describe it. No gentle metaphor. It was like watching a train come off the tracks in real time.

His whole world jerked sideways.

All he heard was that I'd been asked to claim another man's baby. That my name was tied to some scandal, some so-called affair that wasn't real but sounded real enough to blow up trust.

He left.

I watched him pick himself up and walk out of the life we built, straight into his uncle's house. Away from me. Away from what we were.

I was left with Levi

And pregnant.

Alone.

Again.

But this time it wasn't some random disaster or a bad man with a weapon or a wrong-place-wrong-time story.

It was my dad.

Back in my life, swinging wrecking balls like nothing had changed.

I was so devastated I didn't even have a word for it.

There's a kind of heartbreak that makes you cry,
text your friends, listen to sad music.

And then there's the kind that makes you stop
caring if you make it home.

I walked down the middle of the road.

Not on the shoulder.
Not on the sidewalk.
Dead center.

I wasn't drunk.
I wasn't high.

I was just done.

Done being a pawn.
Done being the sacrifice.
Done having my life torched every time my dad wanted
something fixed.

Some ugly, quiet part of me hoped a car would
come flying around the corner and not see me.

Just... lights, impact, silence.

I didn't want to be here anymore. Not if "here"
meant watching my life go from fun adventures and
building something real — to this:

The same man who'd already ruined my childhood
walking right back into my world and demolishing what
I'd rebuilt as an adult.

People talk about "breaking generational curses"
like it's a Pinterest quote.

What they don't talk about is what it feels like the
day you realize the curse still knows where you live.

And it just took out your future with one phone call.

CHAPTER NINE

Pick a Life, Any Life

***

A couple months went by, and I still was messed up. Everything with the attorney blew up, the storm finally started to die down.

Cases got closed. Papers got filed. People went quiet

I didn't wait around for the ending. I pulled myself out of that whole mess like a hand out of boiling water. I wanted no part of it, no more letting my dad use my life as a legal sacrifice.

I wanted my family back.

And if I couldn't have that, I at least wanted a life that was mine.

So, I did something I thought I would never do, especially someone with my past:

I enrolled in college.

Still pregnant and wrecked.
Still carrying a heart that felt like it had been hit by a train.

I figured if I couldn't fix what had already happened, I could at least prove I was worthy of something.

A degree and worthy of a future.

Worthy of more than whatever my dad decided I was good for that week.

I went to classes. I did the work. I walked through halls full of kids who looked younger and freer than I ever got to be and tried not to think about how late I was showing up to this version of life.

When I wasn't in class or home with Levi, I started walking in the woods.

Just to get out of those empty walls and away from the echo of all the yelling that had happened in my life. Trees didn't ask questions. Squirrels didn't care about my GPA. The woods were the only place that didn't expect anything from me except that I keep breathing.

Some days, that was a stretch.

One of those walks, I noticed a rash on my ankle.

It looked weird. But I was pregnant, stressed, and had seen my body do plenty of strange stuff already. I shrugged it off.

Big, stupid mistake number one-thousand and something.

I started getting sick.

Not "I threw up once and took a nap" sick.

Sick. Sick.

That intense sick that feels like your bones are trying to dissolve and your organs are running their own protest.

I ended up in the hospital.

Lines. Monitors. Nurses speaking in that specific tone people use when they're trying not to worry you, which is exactly how you know you should be worried.

Jeff came to see me.

Walking into that room, he wasn't the guy who'd left for his uncle's. He wasn't the Jeff from the pond nights, either. He was somewhere in between hurt, confused, still carrying the wreckage of what my dad had forced between us.

We talked.

Slowly. Awkwardly at first, like strangers with matching memories.

Somewhere between the IV drips and the blood draws, we started to heal a little. Not magically. Not "forgive and forget." Just... ***okay, we're still here, somehow.***

For a minute, it felt like we were going to make it out of this chapter alive.

Then my body decided to raise the stakes.

I became bedridden.

My blood pressure tanked, my body went into crisis mode. And we started losing the baby.

We found out she was a girl.

A girl.

Those two words hit me harder than any diagnosis.

All my past came roaring back at once, the little me in court, the name change, the quiet deals, the screams no one wanted to hear. The idea of bringing a daughter into a world that had already done what it did to me?

I was terrified.

My body was failing. My mind was spinning. My heart was somewhere between "I can't do this" and "I have to do this right."

I went into labor early.

Still sick. Still weak. Machines blinking around me like a Christmas tree nobody asked for.

We raced to the hospital.

At some point, the medical staff made it very clear: this wasn't going to be a simple "push, cry, cut the cord" situation.

It came down to a choice.

Me.

Or her.

They put that decision in Jeff's hands.

He knew what the doctors knew: saving both of us wasn't guaranteed.

And thanks to my dad and his little nuclear bomb of a lie, there was a thought already lodged in his brain:

This probably isn't even my kid.

Big shoutout to my father for that, really. Hell of a legacy.

So when they asked Jeff who to save, he did what scared men do when they've been lied to and broken:

He chose me.

Save her.

The safer bet. The known quantity. The one he had history with.

When I heard that, even half delirious and half dying, I said *"no"*

"Save her."

I meant it with everything I had left.

If only one of us was walking out of that room, it was going to be her.

I was thinking about all the chances I never got.

I was thinking about breaking curses.

I was just tired of always being the one who survived."

Whatever it was, I chose her.

They listened.

And somehow — by skill, by luck, by sheer stubbornness — we both made it.

She lived.

I lived.

Afterward, they moved me back to my hospital room. I was wrecked — physically, emotionally, spiritually, whatever other boxes exist. I'd just walked the line between life and death with my daughter in my arms and this man standing at the edge of the whole thing.

You'd think this would be one of those moments where everyone goes quiet and grateful.

Instead, Jeff looked right at me and said:

"See ya later. I'll pick you up when you get out. I'm not missing my birthday celebration at the bar with my buddies."

I had just nearly died.

Our daughter had just nearly died.

I was lying there, stitched, and fragile and holding the tiny human both of us had almost lost—

and he was worried about missing shots at the bar.

I didn't yell.

I didn't cry.

I just... *knew.*

In that moment, I saw it crystal clear:

What my dad had done, what he'd forced me to lie about, had cut Jeff so deep it never healed right. It healed crooked. It healed infected. It healed around this idea that nothing with me could ever be trusted again.

The man who once threw another man out of my house for hurting me...
was now leaving me in a hospital bed to go celebrate his birthday like none of this had happened.

I watched him walk out.

And somewhere deep inside, a quiet part of me said:

Okay. That's who you are now.

The doctors saved my life.
I saved my daughter's.

Somewhere in the middle of all that, I lost whatever version of Jeff I thought would always choose us first.

CHAPTER TEN

Palm Trees, Panic & Two Very Different Kids

*****

$\mathcal{T}$he next few years were palm trees, panic, and survival math—until we came back to Michigan.

When Sarah was a newborn and we were trying to build a life with palm trees, and trying to be a normal family again, silence started sounding wrong to me.

The day we brought Sarah home, quiet didn't feel like rest anymore; it felt like a warning.

She didn't come with the standard baby package.

Right out of the gate, she had seizures. She'd randomly stop breathing. And her development ran on a schedule that apparently only she and God understood.

Other moms filled baby books with "first smile" and "first rollover."

Mine looked like: Didn't die today. Turned pink again. Only scared the nurses half to death this week.

Every time she got quiet, I wasn't thinking, "Aww, she's resting."

I was thinking,

Is she breathing, or do I need to flip her like a pancake and call 911 again?

I didn't hover because I was paranoid. I hovered because I learned the hard way that quiet can be dangerous. I'd lean over her crib and watch for the smallest rise of her chest, counting seconds like they were beads on a rosary. My ears stayed tuned to sounds other parents never had to listen for: the pause, the change, the wrong kind of stillness.

And then I'd look at my son and feel the whiplash of parenting two worlds at once.

Levi—the cartoon character coming to life.

Bright. Loud. Fast.

He woke up like an alarm that someone threw across the room and just kept going.

If there was something to jump off, he was airborne.

If there was a "don't touch," his fingerprints were already on it.

If there was a clean outfit, he fixed that.

So daily life was:

One child I was terrified would stop moving.

One child I was terrified would never stop moving.

I'd be hovering over Sarah's chest, counting breaths, while yelling, *"LEVI, GET OFF THAT. WE DO NOT CLIMB THE FRIDGE,"* in the same sentence.

I wasn't a stay-at-home mom. I was a full-time crisis manager.

Time did what time does: ignored my feelings and kept going.

Slowly, the sharp panic filled itself down to dull panic. Sarah grew. The seizures and breathing scares didn't vanish, but they stopped happening every five seconds. Levi at five still remained a human pinball, but at least I knew his style.

We found something that almost looked like a rhythm. A chaotic, off-beat, probably-concerning rhythm—but it was ours.

Then the background changed.

Palm trees.

Ocean.

California.

Jeff's job landed us on a year-long contract out there, and just like that, our circus got a better backdrop.

We packed up the kids, the medical records, the bills, the trauma, and whatever was left of our sanity, then pointed the car west.

We traded snowbanks for sand.

Salt trucks for saltwater.

People who knew our business for people who didn't know us at all.

And I was safe.

It wasn't magically healed.

Because there were finally miles between us and the people and places that kept blowing us up.

It was like emotional witness protection with better weather.

California wasn't some fairytale. But it felt like breathing with both lungs for once.

Levi discovered palm trees you couldn't climb (he tried).

Sarah found specialists who didn't look at me like I was crazy when I said, "She just stops breathing sometimes."

I found grocery stores where nobody side-eyed me like,

"didn't you used to be that girl from..".

For a second, I let my shoulders drop.

This.

This felt like home.

Not childhood home. Not legal mailing address home.

Chosen home.

No one is popping in with history.

No one dropping off threats disguised as "family."

Just us, our mess, and the ocean.

If trauma had a volume knob, California turned it down a couple notches.

I finally thought:

We did it. We outran the bullshit.

I let myself believe it for a full minute. So of course, that's when the contract ended.

One day Jeff had a job.

The next day, we were looking at each other like:

"So... how attached are we to paying bills?"

California is fun. California is pretty.

California is also expensive as hell when the paychecks stop.

So we had to do the thing we were now unintentionally good at:

Pack up. Again.

The only thing keeping that from breaking me completely was this:

While we were in California, we'd done something that almost felt illegal for people like us.

We bought a house in Michigan.

On paper, it sounded backwards:

We finally get palm trees and buy property in the land of black ice and potholes.

But it made sense in our heads.

We wanted a place that was ours.

No landlord. No "you've got 30 days." No "my name is on your disaster."

A house to raise our kids in.

A place we could finally call home permanently, even if we were temporarily playing in the sunshine.

We picked a medium sized town where:

1. The schools were small.
2. The neighbors weren't all up in your business unless you were all up in theirs.
3. The towns people left you alone unless you went hunting for attention.

Perfect.

So when the California contract died, we loaded up the family again — one medically-fragile warrior girl, one feral golden retriever boy in human form, two exhausted semi-functioning adults—

and headed back across the country.

This time, we weren't just going "back to Michigan."

We were driving toward something we'd never really had:

A house with our name on it.

A town that didn't know our whole history.

A chance, at least on paper, at an actual stable home.

And for a minute — just a minute—

it felt like we'd finally built something life couldn't just snatch away.

Spoiler: life heard that and said "Bet."

CHAPTER ELEVEN

Guano Happens

***

*B*ack in Michigan, the house started filling with things we couldn't see. But this time it wasn't our house.

This wasn't my Christmas Eve. It was Jeff's friend Dave's, and it pulled me into a fight I wasn't willing to ignore.

Christmas Eve is supposed to smell like cinnamon rolls, candy canes, and kids ripping wrapping paper like tiny raccoons.
Instead, Dave and his girlfriend got a Christmas Eve that rewires your nervous system.

Her youngest — two years old — went into a seizure for no reason anyone could explain.
He'd been congested. They'd been doing the doctor appointments. Everyone was assuming RSV because winter has a schedule and it never misses.

But when that seizure hit, the doctors stopped guessing and started interrogating the environment:
Any toxins in the home?
Any mold, chemicals, pests, animal droppings, any unusual smells, roof leaks,
any exposure you can think of?

And like most renters who are just trying to keep their kids alive — and their bills paid — they answered the only way you can answer when you don't own the walls around you:

No.

Not that we know of.

Then they brought him home.

That night… bats were flying around inside their house.

Not outside. Not "we saw one near the porch." Inside.

Just looping the living room like they were part of the lease agreement.

When you're a parent with a baby who almost died hours earlier, your brain doesn't go, "Interesting wildlife."

Your brain goes:

This is connected. This is the answer.

They were renting the house. So she contacted the landlord with the doctors' questions.

Of course, the landlord's answers were all "no."

Nothing to see here.

That's the thing about "no" when it comes from the person collecting your money:

it's rarely information. It's a strategy.

Dave went to investigate the attic.

Before he even opened the pull-down ladder, he noticed a black substance around the frame.

Not "dust."

Not "old house grime."

Black.

The black that makes your body understand something before your mind can finish the sentence.

He opened it.

What they found would surprise anyone.

An entire colony of bats living upstairs.

Bat guano everywhere.

Not "a little."

Not "some."

Everywhere.

Suddenly, the baby's lungs, the seizure, the doctor's questions — everything had a possible answer that made everyone sick to their stomachs.

They told the landlord what any normal person should hear and immediately handle:

Removal. Remediation. A plan. A safe home.

The landlord told them they had to pay to remove the bats.

At the same time, their stove was broken.

At the same time, her income was broken.

At the same time, she had two small children and nowhere else to go.

She did the one thing renters are told they're allowed to do in theory — but punished for doing in real life:

She went to put the rent in escrow until the home was safe.

And the landlord proceeded with eviction.

Because slumlords don't fear God or the courts.

The Fine Print Nobody Reads

Here's the part people like to skip:

the moment right after the crisis when nothing is "happening" … but everything is.

Because the emergency isn't the only thing that matters.

It's what comes next.

It's the shrug.

It's the loophole.

It's the "civil matter."

It's the system looking at a threatened child and saying, "We don't do that here."

And that's where I come in.

Because they came to me.

Two kids potentially out on the street because a landlord wouldn't handle something dangerous.

A baby's life threatened, and adults with titles acting like we were debating a fence line.

I don't know how to explain what happens to me in moments like that except this:

I don't calm down.

I become a project.

I went into action the way I used to when I was doing legal work — research mode, binder mode, don't-make-me-pull-out-documents mode.

Because if I didn't do something, I'd start doing math.

Math is dangerous.

Math is where you start adding up:

how many families are one rent payment away from a tent,

how many "no issue" homes are health hazards,

how many kids are breathing things they shouldn't,

how often "no jurisdiction" really means "not our problem."

Exhibit A: The Myth of "No Issues"

Landlords love one phrase more than they love passive income:

"No issues."

Translation: "No issues" doesn't mean there are no issues.

It means there's no paper trail.

No inspection.

No documentation.

No accountability.

And renters are trained to doubt themselves first. They think:

It's normal.

It's an old house.

I'm overreacting.

I can't afford to make trouble.

Meanwhile, bats are living over your head like they own shares in the place.

Exhibit B: The Fix That Isn't a Fix

After the bat situation, you'd think the response would be straightforward.

You'd think we'd have systems designed for "child safety" and "basic health standards."

But what I found was a lot of official-sounding versions of:

"That's unfortunate."

"We don't inspect existing dwellings."

"Our hands are tied."

Or my personal favorite:

"We can condemn the home."

Which sounds responsible until you realize
"condemn" is just a professional way of saying:
We can take away your only shelter for your safety.
Good luck.

Accountability isn't a microwave.
You don't press 30 seconds, hear a beep, and suddenly
everyone's safe and housed.

But that's what people want — fast solutions that
don't disturb anyone with money.

What Made Me Decide to Fight

Once I started digging, other renters came forward.
And once renters come forward, you learn real fast that
"bad luck" has an address.

I started hearing about:

Extension cords being used as permanent wiring.
Septic backups and no working toilets (disabled
children using a tub).
Renters paying repair bills because the landlord refused
— then being threatened with eviction if they tried to
deduct it from rent.
Families begging for help while agencies shrugged and
said, "We don't inspect existing dwellings."

And the pattern was always the same:
People with money got options.
People without money got lectures.

I took it personally.

Because I recognized the system.
I'd watched systems fail people before — quietly,
politely, with a smile and a rule book.

I wasn't going to watch it happen to families who
didn't have the time, words, or energy to fight back.

My New Boundary

My old boundary (in life, in work, in everything) used to be:

"I'm going to explain this until you understand."

That is not a boundary.

That is a hostage negotiation.

My new boundary became:

If you dodge it, I document it.

If you dismiss it, I go public.

Those are boundaries that starve denial.

I realized something that offended me deeply:

Some people don't want clarity.

They want control.

And control hates documentation.

The Dangerous Folder

People call it "being dramatic."

I call it accuracy.

So, I made a folder — photos, testimonies, dates, conditions.

A portfolio that couldn't be shrugged off with a smirk.

Because when you live in a world where the truth gets rewritten like a group project, you start collecting proof like you're in court.

And yes, I know how that sounds.

But if you've ever heard "That never happened," while you can still feel it in your ribs...

you get it.

That portfolio wasn't for attention.

It was for the part of me that refused to gaslight myself.

It was for the renters who kept being told they were

"complaining."
It was for the kids who didn't get a vote.

The Meetings

It took me two months just to get a township meeting.
Two months.
Which is impressive when you consider how quickly they can schedule a meeting to argue about a pothole that's been there since flip phones.
Most of the township members were landlords.
So to get on the minutes, I had to approach it as a "concerned resident."
I played nice.
They bit.
And then I walked in with my portfolio.
Pictures.
Testimonies.
Conditions.
Patterns.
When I finished, the room looked different.
Shoulders sinking.
Chairs suddenly feeling smaller.
Because it's easy to debate policy.
It's harder to debate photos of unsafe living conditions while you pretend you didn't know.
That month, I got invited to the county commissioner's meeting.
So, I didn't show up with feelings.
I showed up with solutions.
I called surrounding counties and asked what they used to keep rental properties safe.

That's when I was directed to the International Property Maintenance Code.

And I read the whole thing.

Cover to cover.

Like a lunatic.

Like someone who finally understood: the system only respects you when you speak in its language.

The key point was this:

Because there were under 100,000 residents, the county didn't have to adopt the entire code.

They could select what fit.

They could set minimum standards.

They could protect people without turning into a bureaucracy.

I walked into that county meeting like I owned the place.

When they called me up, I laid copies of my portfolio in front of every commissioner — pictures, inserts, and recommended code sections.

The building inspector said, confidently, that there was nothing in the building codes requiring inspection of existing dwellings.

He said it like it was checkmate.

So, I pulled out the code book and read the insert I already knew he'd pretend didn't exist.

He sat down.

I continued.

By the end, six out of seven commissioners agreed to a special public meeting with the township so landlords could address concerns.

Public.

That word matters.

Private is where people get ignored.

Public is where people get results.

I ran that meeting — addressing local concerns, hashing out pros and cons, pushing for the minimum safety standards that should've existed the whole time.

The Win (And the Part That Still Stings)

A local agency approached me and asked for permission to use my presentation to fight for grants — improving homes and helping residents get real results.

I said yes.

It would be an honor.

Because my goal wasn't applause.

My goal was: kids not breathing bat waste in a rental house while everyone shrugs.

I also added more evidence and more concerns into their package — because it wasn't one landlord. It was a pattern.

In the end, the agency secured $750,000 in grant money.

That was a win for everyone:

Renters got help.

Homeowners got help.

Conditions improved.

And some townships adapted portions of the code.

And me?

I got the satisfaction of feeling claimed for a moment — because I knew I did something that mattered.

Then the articles came out.

My name wasn't in them.

For the townships, the zoning officers were credited.

For the agency, there was a huge article and even a plaque sitting in a lobby — congratulating the team for the fastest results helping the community.

That plaque didn't have my name on it.

If you've lived my kind of life, you know why that hurts in a specific way.

It's not about ego.

It's about the pattern.

It's about always being the engine and never being the driver.

It's about doing the work and then being painted like you're lying when you talk about it.

All I have are the articles.

And the memory of commissioners sinking into their chairs when they finally realized what was happening in their own towns.

Once again, something I built got claimed by people who didn't build it.

What No One Knew Yet

While I was fighting that battle, I was getting sick. Quietly. Slowly.

The sick that waits until you finish saving everyone else and then steps forward like:

"Okay. Now it's your turn."

I was about to fight another battle.

CHAPTER TWELVE

Exit Ramp

***

A years after fighting for the for better housing we finally got settled into our house— the 'we're not going anywhere' kind—I let myself believe that.
And the second I believed it… my body reminded me who's always been in charge.

We were finally on top of our world, so obviously life had questions.

Jeff was driving truck and, for once, it felt like we had it made

We had the house.

Not just a house.

The house.

Heated swimming pool.
Generator hardwired in, an end-of-the-world ready, but make it comfortable

A full basement with bedrooms.
Central air.
A big front yard with a rolling hill that looked like the opening shot of a "happy family" commercial I never thought I'd star in.

It was a setup where people scroll past on Zillow and think, *Must be nice.*

Somehow, it was ours.

For a minute, I actually let the thought in:

We did it. We survived all that shit and landed here.

My stomach rolled the second I believed it. So of course, my body said, "Hold my beer."

I started getting sick, Jeff was out on the road. He was out there, living a whole separate life I didn't know about.

At first it was just tired, off, run-down. I'd been through enough that "not feeling great" barely registered. I thought I was just over doing it but pushed myself for these families.

Then "off" turned into wrong.

He was gone more. Over-the-road trucker life isn't just a job; it's a slow leak in your bank account.

Fuel. Food. Maintenance.
And in his case: Vegas-style expenses.

You send a man out on the road long enough and suddenly "expense report" looks a lot like casinos, bars, and "don't ask too many questions."

So, he stayed gone.

Longer runs. More weeks away. Me at home with the kids, getting sicker, while the money we were supposedly making was disappearing into truck stops and neon lights in Vegas

While he was out there living the long-haul life, Dave was the one-stepping in.

Not as a replacement. As a driver.

When I had appointments, Dave was the one taking me.

Doctors. Tests. Waiting rooms that smelled. He sat there. Jeff didn't.

I got diagnosed.
I had surgery.
They said they got it all.
"Good margins. We're optimistic."
Then came the sentence patients and their families
always repeat like it's not loaded:
"We'll just do a little chemo to be sure."
Just... a little.
Like they were talking about sugar in coffee.

Chemo was not "a little."
It wrecked me.
I was sick through the whole thing.
My bones hurt. My teeth hurt. My hair hated me.
My organs were filing HR complaints.
Everything tasted like metal and regret.
I lived in a rotation of bed, bathroom, and the parts of
the house I could reach without collapsing.
Two kids needed a mom.
What they had was a woman trying to survive
poison while the husband who'd said "in sickness and
in health" was mostly married to the highway.
Levi was nine.

Sarah was seven.
That was the reality
When Jeff came home one day, walked in like it
was any other day, and dropped this:
"We're done. I'm moving out."

No warning or build-up.
 Not even a "Hey, we should talk to someone before I blow our lives up again."

Just — delivery:
We're done. I'm out.
He swore it wasn't another woman
Like that was the part I was relieved about.
Great.
So you're not leaving me for someone else, you're just leaving me.

He didn't just leave *me*.
He left for another woman.
All that "it's not another woman" crap?
Yeah. That was a lie with a steering wheel attached.

While I was home with chemo brain — another "unplugged halfway through her download" moment — he was out there picking her up in his semi and hauling her right out of town with him.

I was throwing up poison and he was playing long-haul lover boy.

He left our nine-year-old to take care of me.
He left Dave to drive me to appointments.

Levi became the man of the house because the actual man of the house decided he'd rather be a tour guide for his side piece.

My son — nine years old — had to help me bathe.

I wore a swimsuit so he wouldn't see me naked. He was still a kid. But it didn't matter how much fabric I put between us, the shame was still there.

The shame wasn't about him, it was that my child was paying a price for an adult man's absence.
Shame in the situation.

Shame in being the mom who couldn't physically take care of herself. Shame in letting this boy see, way too early, just how fragile his mother really was.

While I was fighting to stay alive, another fear started nagging at me:

If I lose this battle...
Where do my kids go?
Who ends up in charge of them?

Because the man who walked away from me during chemo was still legally the man who has a say.

So I had to fight.

For my life.
For theirs.
And quietly, for what was left of my sanity.

As if cancer wasn't enough, the house started slipping away too.

Foreclosure crept in like mold — slow at first, then all at once.

Payments got behind. Fees stacked up. Letters showed up with words like "default" and "sale date" and "final notice."

There were options.
I could've tried to save it. Work something out. Modify, negotiate, claw it back from the edge.

But I couldn't do any of that without him.

His name was on it.
His signature was required.

And Jeff?

Refused.

It was like watching someone stand there with a fire extinguisher while your house is burning and saying,

"Nah. Gotta let it go."

So there I was:

Sick.

On chemo.

With chemo-brain.

Two kids.

And a house sliding into foreclosure because the man who helped build it would rather let it die than work with me to fix it.

I was too weak to physically fight and too legally trapped to fix it alone.

I thought that was the bottom.

Then he showed back up.

He didn't come back with an apology.

He came back with leverage.

My stomach dropped.

This man walked in and told me he'd been talking to my dad.

Of all people my dad.

Of course.

My pulse thudded in my ears. He even had my dad on the phone.

Just what every chemo patient wants: The man that walked out on me and her abuser teaming up like some kind of special episode of "How Much Worse Can This Get?"

They had a plan.

I wasn't to save the house.

Not to help the kids.

Not to make anything right.

To take.

Threaten.

And control.

Jeff looked at me and basically laid out the terms like a debt collector:

I had to give up my 1978 Y88 Trans Am—

or my dad was going to "help" take the kids.

It wasn't a suggest.

Not imply.

Help him.

They both knew exactly where my weak point was.

I was sick.

I was damaged.

I was in chemo.

My brain was still glitching.

And there was a real possibility that if this went to court, with my health, my meds, my history, someone could twist it and make me look unfit.

I knew how the system worked and I knew how my dad worked

I helped fight to protect kids and the parents

This didn't matter.

On paper, in that moment, I was vulnerable.

So, it was a no-brainer.

My kids or my car?

My kids, every time.

It was not just money. It was me buying my kids distance from my father, one sacrifice at a time.

I handed over the Trans Am.

My Limited Edition, one of the few things in my life that had ever been *mine* and not tied to somebody else's bad choices. The car got sacrificed to keep my children out of my dad's hands and out of court.

They walked away with the car.

I stayed with the kids.

It was the right choice.

It still felt like being robbed at gunpoint.

So: cancer took my health.
Foreclosure took my house.
He took my car.
And my dad was still, somehow, in the middle of my life, pulling strings.

But I was still standing.

Barely.
Angry.
Sick.
Humiliated.

And somewhere under all that, a new version of me was forming:

The woman who now understood, very clearly, that nobody was coming to save her.

Not husbands.
Not dads.

Not men in uniforms.

Not men in suits.

If I was going to make it out with my kids, my sanity, and whatever was left of my soul—

it was going to be because *I* did it.

Again.

But before the paperwork, the threats, and the scrambling to keep my kids' world steady – I need to take you back a step—to what was going on inside of me and around me that I had no control over.

The call you can't ignore.

CHAPTER THIRTEEN

What Chemo Looked Like Behind Closed Doors

***

That year I used to think the worst part of my life would be always doing things alone while my husband was gone.

A hard-working man leaving for months at a time.

It ended with a man making promises like they were coupons that expired the second you tried to use them.

Turns out the worst part of my life wasn't the hard working man leaving in the end.

It didn't slam a door.

It didn't pack a bag.

It didn't even have the decency to announce itself dramatically.

It showed up like junk mail.

At first it was little stuff.

Tired — but the tired that didn't match the day I had.

It made me sit down to "rest for a second," and then realize it was dark outside.

Like I'd missed a whole piece of my own life.

I blamed stress.

Because stress is the most convenient lie in the world. You can put anything under it:

- headaches
- stomach pain
- sleeplessness
- body aches

• weird appetite
• numbness
• panic
• exhaustion
• rage
• crying in the laundry room at 2 a.m. because the dryer beep sounded judgmental

Stress is the explanation that makes everyone nod and move along.

No one argues with stress.

And I didn't have time for anything that required time.

The first time I let myself wonder if it was something else, I did the thing I always do.

I tried to talk myself out of it.

"Maybe I'm just run down."

"I'm dehydrated."

"I'm not eating right."

"I'm depressed."

"It's my hormones."

"Maybe I'm turning into one of those people who can feel the weather in their knees."

The real truth:

If you grew up in my world, you don't go to the doctor when something feels wrong.

You wait until your body turns the check engine light into a full fireworks show.

Then you go — and you apologize for it like you're inconveniencing everyone.

Pain, I can manage.

Fear, I can swallow.

Symptoms, I can ignore.

But your body will only let you ignore it for so long before it starts speaking in capital letters.

By the time I made the appointment, it wasn't brave.

It was practical.

I didn't go because I suddenly loved myself and respected my health.

I went because I had kids.

And because something in me told me to fight. That whisper of: "You don't get to disappear. Not yet."

So I showed up the way I show up for everything: Tired. Broke. Pretending I wasn't scared.

The waiting room smelled like disinfectant and old magazines.

The nurse asked questions in that casual tone that makes you forget they're collecting evidence.

Any family history?

Any symptoms?

How long have you felt this?

Have you noticed changes?

I answered like I was reciting a grocery list. Because if I said it like it mattered, I might fall apart right there between the flu posters and the outdated pamphlets about cholesterol.

Then the tests started.

And the thing about tests is they don't feel like they're testing your body.

They feel like they're testing your ability to remain a person while strangers calmly rearrange your reality.

Go here.

Sit there.

Hold still.
Breathe in.
Breathe out.
Don't move.
Wait.

"We'll call you."

That phrase should be illegal.
Because "we'll call you" is what people say right
before your life splits into before and after.

Waiting, is where my mind goes feral.
Waiting, is where every memory I've ever had shows
up like it heard there were snacks.

I tried to keep things normal.
School runs.
Dinner.
Meds.
Laundry.

The TV stayed on too loud again, because quiet still
felt dangerous.
And at night, after the kids were down, I'd sit on that
same couch and stare at that same stack of letters and
pretend it was all manageable if I didn't look at it too
hard.

I felt myself wanting to do what I always do:
Detach.
Leave my body.
Float above it like it was happening to another woman.

But then I'd hear one of my kids cough down the
hall, or I'd picture Sarah needing her meds, or Levi
needing me to sign something, and I'd snap back into
myself.

No. Stay here. Stay here.

Because being a mom doesn't stop just because you're terrified.

Trauma doesn't pause life.

Life just keeps asking you to pack lunches anyway.

The call came at the worst possible time.

Which is always.

There's never a good time for:

"Hello, this is the doctor's office."

It's never when you're fresh and hydrated and emotionally stable, sitting in a sunlit room with a support person and a blanket.

No.

It's always when your phone is on 2 percent, one kid is yelling about something sticky, and you're already tired from trying not to spiral.

I answered.

And the voice on the other end did that careful tone.

The tone that tells you the news has teeth.

They started speaking — words, facts, terms — and my body tried to leave again.

The old reflex.

The old escape hatch.

But this time I grabbed onto something.

Not strength.

Not positivity.

Not "God's plan."

I grabbed onto spite.

Because spite is free.

And in that moment, I remember thinking:

Are you kidding me?
You mean to tell me I survived my father, the system,
the group homes, the courtroom, that label…
Just to get taken out by my own cells?
No.
Absolutely not.
After the call, everything turned into a list.
That's how my brain handles terror.
It turns fear into tasks.
Appointments.
Referrals.
Paperwork.
Transportation.
Insurance.
Money I didn't have.
Time I didn't have.
And the weirdest part is people think the hardest
part is hearing the diagnosis.
It isn't.
The hardest part is the next morning when your kid
says, "What's for breakfast?" like nothing happened.
You have to answer like a normal human.
Because your child's world is still pancakes and
cartoons.
Your world just became a life or death situation.
You do what moms do.
You make breakfast.
You smile.
You crack a joke.
You swallow the scream.
And you keep moving.

At home, nothing stopped.
Bills still came.
The foreclosure letters didn't care about my diagnosis.
They didn't soften their tone.
They didn't pause for compassion.
They kept arriving like demands:
Pay.
Fix.
Respond.
Prove it.
Comply.
And still, bedtime happened.
Sarah needed her routine and her meds.
Levi needed a laugh and some sign the world wasn't
about to collapse.
So I performed "Mom" like it was a paid position
with no sick days.
Blankets up.
Forehead kisses.
"You're safe."
I said it like a spell.
If I'm being honest, I didn't always believe it.
But I said it anyway because kids deserve certainty
even when their mother is swallowing fear like
vitamins.
Then I'd walk back out into the living room and feel
the quiet creep in.
That's when the old logic tried to take over again.
"See? This is what happens to girls like you."
"Too much."

"Too broken."

"Too…"

And for once, something new answered back.

Not sweet, healing or inspirational.

Just clear.

It's not you.

It's what you've been carrying.

Something about getting sick doesn't make you enlightened.

It makes you allergic to bullshit.

If I could pretend this chapter ends with some clean moral, I would.

But the truth is, at this point in my life, I wasn't learning big inspirational lessons.

I was learning smaller, meaner truths:

Your body will keep score even when your mouth stays quiet.

Not everyone knows how to stay when life stops being fun.

The system does not care if you're sick. It only cares if you're late.

Love isn't proven in good times. It's proven when your life is ugly and inconvenient.

And still, under all of it, something stubborn was growing.

Not hope.

Hope felt too soft for this part of the story.

This was closer to refusal — refusing to let the universe finish the job, and refusing to let my kids watch me disappear the way I **used to** disappear inside myself.

A refusal to let old memories write the ending for me.

And now, after the call, I could feel it:
Healing wasn't going to show up as a moment.
It was going to show up as a decision I made over and over.

To stay.
To speak.
To fight.

To stop handing my worth to people who could drop it.

Because after the call, after the tests, after the news that had teeth…
I didn't become a softer woman.
I became a clearer one.

Clear enough to stop explaining my pain to people who benefited from my silence.

CHAPTER FOURTEEN

Veggie Brain & the Scheduled Boyfriend

***

 $\mathcal{T}$he following summer, my brain wasn't the

same—and neither was my definition of "normal."

My brain was not at full capacity. It was running on emergency power and sarcasm — barely enough to keep the lights on. Which is exactly when I made the most me decision possible: I added one more complication and called it hope.

Nine months after *the call*, life didn't slow down or soften.

The house was still doing its regular noises — the refrigerator humming, the furnace clicking on and off, the mail sliding onto the counter — like it didn't realize our whole life was being packed into the spaces between those sounds.

Just me, Levi, and Sarah sitting in a house we were going to lose, watching the date creep closer to a tent.

Every time I walked through a room, I was mentally packing.

 What can I fit in a car? What must stay? Where are we even going?

And I didn't become softer when everything collapsed.

I became clearer — and my clarity did what it always

does when I'm terrified:

It tried to move.

In the middle of foreclosure, chemo fog, single parenting, and emotional bankruptcy, I decided to do the most me thing possible.

I went back to college again.

Still chemo fogged. Still exhausted. Still half unplugged like my brain was buffering on dial-up. But I was trying. God was I trying.

I'd sit in class, and the teacher would start talking about common sense, common denominators, common anything... and my brain would just slide right off it.

I could do trauma math just fine:

> Dad + court = new name
>
> Jeff + dad + lies = disaster
>
> Men + my life = structural damage

But anything on the whiteboard?

Chemo brain said: *We're closed. Try again later.*

And then, because apparently, I hadn't suffered enough, I decided:

You know what this life tornado needs?

A man.

I met someone.

At first, I thought I might be ready. Which was adorable in hindsight.

This guy's idea of romance?

Scheduling.

Not, "Hey, when are you free?"

No.

It was:

"Don't call me until Wednesday. I'll tell you what day you can come over."

I stared at my phone like it had just insulted my mother.

"... Sir, are you asking me out, or onboarding me as an employee?"

I'd been out of the dating game for a while, so for half a second I wondered if this was normal now. "Does affection comes with appointment slots and confirmation emails?"

But even with veggie brain, I had enough sense to squint at it.

I stopped seeing him, because I wasn't ready... and because everything about him felt like a Terms & Conditions screen I should've hit "Decline" on.

Eventually, loneliness teamed up with chemo fog and said:

"Let's try it. How bad could it be?"

When I finally went, it felt wrong.

Not dangerous wrong — just *off.*

Like wearing a shirt that technically fits but makes your soul itch.

The second I walked in, I had that weird feeling like I was doing something wrong — It wasn't because I was cheating on anyone, but because I was betraying myself.

He was an alcoholic with "boundaries."

Now, there are real, healthy boundaries.

And then there are:

"Don't call until Wednesday. I'll tell you when you're allowed to exist again."

These were the second kind.

He wasn't deep, complicated, layered, or intense.

He was flat.

Like a soda left open for two days.

Like hospital Jell-O.

Just... there.

No wild, stupid ideas.

No laughing until your stomach hurt.

No "let's go live before we die."

Nothing.

It was like hanging out with a human beige wall who thought he was a catch because he owned a clock.

If I'd had my full brain online, I would've pulled out a notebook and written:

Things To Never Date Again:

Alcoholic with a spreadsheet brain

Schedules my feelings

Confuses control with "boundaries"

Has the emotional range of a folding chair

But chemo had my mental assistant on vacation, so instead of studying him like a red-flag specimen, I just... went with it.

Because on top of his lack of emotion, I had veggie brain.

Iconic combo.

Eventually, the scheduling thing lit my last nerve on fire.

Nothing in my life has ever been organized.

The only time I've lived on strict schedules with harsh rules was my childhood—
and I sure as hell wasn't signing up for Season Two under some dude with a calendar and a drinking problem.

He'd say:

"Don't call me today."

"I'll let you know when I'm free."

"We'll talk on Wednesday."

Meanwhile I'm sitting there like:

I've survived a violent ex, my dad, courtrooms, cancer, chemo, and foreclosure...
and now this man thinks I'm going to sit by a phone like it's 1952 waiting for King Happy Hour to grant me permission to speak?

Absolutely not.

I am many things.

I am a messed up and broken.

I am tired.

I lose my keys and sometimes my words.

But I am not:

A time slot

A reschedulable activity

A Wednesday-only subscription

If he needed boundaries, he should've put them around his liquor, his trauma, and his control issues — not around my ability to dial a phone like I was applying for visitation.

The more he barked rules, the more the old me woke up.

Not the soft, begging version.

The one that lit clothes on fire in the yard.
The one that crawled with a frying pan.
The one that told a man, "Don't fall asleep," after he stabbed her. That girl does not ask a man:
"Sorry, is this an approved time to feel wanted?"

So no, it didn't last.

It wasn't a tragic breakup.

It was more like:
"Thank you for the demo I'll never be purchasing this model."

Looking back, I don't regret him.

He was a walking lesson.

I still didn't know exactly what I *did* want yet...

But I knew this:

I was done bowing to a man's "rules."
Done letting someone with less courage than me decide when I'm allowed to take up space.
Done mistaking controlling behavior for "structure" or "stability."

If he needed boundaries, he could keep them.

I had my own now.

And none of them involved asking any man when I was allowed to call.
Something I was finally starting to understand—
sometimes your brain will call control "stability" when it's starving for safety. And that's where the ghost logic begins.

CHAPTER FIFTEEN

Ghost Logic

***

That same summer kept twisting logic and playing tricks on me.

Chemo didn't just drain my body — it scrambled my instincts. I wasn't thinking in full sentences; I was thinking in shortcuts and coping mechanisms. And one of my oldest coping mechanisms is mistaking "something new" for "something safe."

Here's my logic: paperwork can feel like a countdown even when nobody is yelling.

Notices that don't make noise. But they fill a house. And when a house fills up with that kind of quiet, you also hear what's missing — no second adult to tag in, no miracle check in the mail — just me, two kids. And a clock ticking down on a home we were going to lose.

Daytime was noisy enough that I could fake it.

School runs. Doctor appointments. Cheap dinners thrown together like a game show challenge. Levi talking a mile a minute. Sarah needing meds, blankets, adjustments. The TV always a little too loud, because quiet felt dangerous.

But once they were in bed, the whole world narrowed down to:

One tired mom.

One stack of mail you don't want to open

One couch that still smelled like sweats and fear from treatment

I'd leave the TV on for company, some sitcom laughing at its own jokes, and stare right through it.

That was when my brain liked to flip through channels I didn't ask for.

Click.

The car in the field.

Upholstery smelling like oil and mold. Windows fogged. My own body gone somewhere else, so I didn't have to be in it. The exact second, I learned you can't always run, so you learn how to leave yourself instead.

Click.

The house of rules.

Chore lists on the fridge. The sound of someone's voice rising in the next room and my stomach dropping before I even understood why. Saying "thank you" with a broken jaw because the rule was: be grateful, even when it hurts.

Click.

The group home kitchen table.

Her in her chair, smug as a cat, saying:

"They would never be with a girl like you."

Like it was just a fact. Like gravity.

Later, years later, me saying "Yeah. Sons," and watching it land like a punch in her throat.

Click.

The courtroom.

Feet not touching the floor. Cold wood under my palms. A judge looking down like he could see the whole story, but only through papers and other people's mouths. My truth laid out in reports, but somehow, I still felt like the one on trial.

Click.

My dad.

His voice on the phone, too calm. His eyes in the rearview mirror when he drove. That mix of charm and threat that always felt like standing on a trapdoor.

By the time the reel ended, I'd still be sitting on my couch in Michigan, TV blinking at me, envelopes stacked on the table.

Two kids asleep down-the-hall, I was terrified I wouldn't be able to keep.

The past didn't stay in the past.
It curled up next to me every night and put its feet on my furniture.

People love neat questions.

"Why did you stay?"
"Why did you pick him?"
"How did you not see it coming?"

Because this is the operating system I was running.

If you grow up being moved like disposable items, you don't learn, ***I have a choice.***

You learn, ***At least I'm being kept.***

If people touch your body and call it love, you don't learn, *My boundaries matter.*

You learn, *If I say no, it'll be worse*
If your life lives in case files and court folders, you don't learn, *My voice counts.*

You learn, *Whatever's on paper wins*
I was a woman, now with a mortgage and two kids, I'm not starting from ground zero anymore
I walked into adulthood pre-programmed:
Be useful.
Be quiet.
Don't need too much.
Take the blame, it's the only way anything makes sense.
That's the control of my past that sat on the arm of the couch every night, watching me fall apart and taking notes.
Adding a layer on top of that was the fact no one ever showed me what a real family looked like when it wasn't pretending.
No couple sat me down and accidentally taught me:
"We love each other and sometimes we fight. But we don't break each other."
I saw doors slammed, things smashing, no silent treatments, never leaving without cops, threats that weren't threats at all, they were actions to resolve the problem at that time
Not two grown adults in the same room, choosing each other on purpose.

The reality is my "how to family" manual came from a TV show.

Somewhere in my brain, there's always been a little black-and-white rerun of *Leave It to Beaver* playing.

June Cleaver in a pressed dress and pearls, somehow always with a clean counter.

Kids arguing over cartoon problems.

Ward walking in from work, taking off his hat, kissing June like it's just what you do at the end of the day.

I knew it was fake.

I knew nobody actually lives like that.

But it looked... **stable**

No cops on the porch.

No social worker popping in.

No garbage bags full of kids 'stuff at the curb in the middle of the night.

No tiptoeing past closed doors wondering if someone was awake and angry.

Just a man who worked hard and kept showing up. A woman who ran the house and wasn't terrified in her own kitchen.

I didn't want to *be* June Cleaver. I wasn't built for pearls and quiet smiling.

But I wanted that backdrop for my kids.

No fighting in front of them.

No adults using their bodies as punching bags or ashtrays or secrets.

No watching their mother disappear into herself because that was safer than speaking.

So, I did what I could with what I had.

I cooked.
I cleaned.

I tried to laugh at his jokes.
 I tried to be grateful, to show appreciation, to make it look like this house, this life, this man, were enough.
If I could just hold up my end, the picture would stay still.

Jeff was the first crack in that old system.
And he didn't only arrive one day with a truck and a tool belt and a grown man's face.
He'd been there since before anybody thought I'd ever make it to "grown woman."
Back when I was bouncing through foster care, counting adults like exits, Jeff was my best friend in high school.
The skinny kid who talked too fast.
Who could annoy me and make me laugh at the same time.
Who walked down crappy linoleum hallways with me like we were two normal teens instead of a foster girl and a boy with his own mess.
Everyone else saw my file.
He saw me.
We weren't some romantic teen movie. We were two kids sitting on stairs, in parking lots, on bleachers — talking about everything and nothing so we didn't have to think about what waited for us at home.
He was the first boy in my life who didn't treat my body like a toy or a weapon.

He just... liked being around me.

So when I ran into him years later at the fair — taller, broader, still machine-gun talking — it didn't feel like meeting a man.

It felt like getting a piece of my own history back that hadn't hurt me.

This time, we didn't just walk and talk.

We built a whole life

He was the one who came into my house and physically threw my ex out.

The one who basically said without saying, "Not on my watch. Not to her. Not again."

For someone like me, that didn't just feel good.

It rewrote something.

We had pond nights, dirty jokes, and those stupid little adventures that make no sense on paper but keep you breathing. We had Levi. We had Sarah. We had bills, arguments, and busy schedules, the full unglamorous package real couples carry.

We had the house.

The hill.

The heated pool.

Central air humming

Kids running through the yard.

My bootleg June Cleaver backdrop.

It wasn't perfect. We weren't perfect.

But for a girl who'd always been the extra kid on someone else's couch, standing in that yard with him felt like screaming at the universe:

Look. I made a real life. You didn't win.

Which is exactly why it felt like such a cruel joke when he left.

He didn't leave a wife.
He left the foster kid who'd trusted him in high school.
The girl who'd believed him when he said he loved her more than the wreckage.
The woman who'd bet her one shot at a "normal" family on him meaning it.
He walked out during cancer.
During chemo.
During foreclosure.
He left for another woman he was picking up in his semi like she was just another load. While our nine-year-old son was at home helping me wash my chemo body in a swimsuit because I couldn't stay standing in the tub.
And my ghost logic slid right into the driver's seat.
See? You're the problem. You're the storm. You're the common denominator.
Didn't matter that my dad had forced that lie.
Didn't matter who really chose what.
Didn't matter how many times I'd shown up and survived things that should have turned me into nothing.
The story in my head lined up like it had been waiting all along:
My lungs forgot how to take a full breath.
Too much.
Too broken.

Too loud.
Too "girl like you."
Of course he left.
Of course it fell apart.
 Of course you're alone again on a couch with overdue notices and kids and a body that doesn't work the way it used to.

The worst part is juggling that and still answering to the name "Mom."
Because while my brain is screening the trauma highlight reel on repeat, life doesn't pause.
Levi comes in, wanting to tell me about a science experiment gone wrong or something some kid said at lunch. Sarah needs help with meds, with sleep, with the lights, with the fan pointed *just right*
They don't need to see the ghosts marching through my head.
They need the version of me that can still make pancakes and terrible jokes.
So I do the thing.
I tuck them in.
Blankets up to their chins.
Kisses on their foreheads.
"You're safe," I tell them.
I say it like a promise, a spell, and a dare to whatever's listening.
I make them laugh.
"Your mom's like a cockroach. I survive everything."

"Even if the house falls down, we'll still be the loudest family on the block."

They giggle.

They don't see the letters on the table.

They don't hear me crying in bed later.

 They don't know how many nights I stand in their doorway thinking:

I will burn this whole world down, before it make you feel as unwanted as I did.

That part's mine.

And then, after they're out cold, I go back to the couch.

Same TV glow.

Same hum of the fridge.

Same stack of bad news.

I start sorting through it all like a junk drawer:

My childhood.

My dad.

The group homes.

 Jeff the boy.

 Jeff the man.

June Cleaver fantasies.

Scheduled boyfriends.

Husbands who leave during head injury and chemo.

It's easy to say, "I should have known better."

It's uglier and truer to admit:

No one ever showed me what "better" even looked like up close

I learned to fight when cornered, freeze when outnumbered, crack jokes when I should be screaming, and move on like nothing happened.

I did not learn:

"You are worth staying for, even when things get hard."

Jeff got closer than anyone to that.
And then he walked.

So now I'm stuck holding this strange double-edge truth:

He was the beginning of my healing—
and living proof that if you hand your healing to another person, they can drop it and walk away.

I wish I could wrap this up with some bumper-sticker moral.

"I chose myself."
"Never questioned my worth again."
"The ghosts moved out."

Easy right? Not even close It was some serious deep thinking.

I started seeing the pattern.

The way I took the blame before anyone asked a question.
The way I wore other people's shame like it was my own coat.
The way I looked at an empty driveway and thought, ***obviously. That makes sense. That's what men do to girls like you.***

Once you see that, you can't unsee it.

You can't instantly fix it either — but you stop mistaking it for the voice of God.

I'm still there, in that house, at the end of this chapter:

Still sick.

Still broke.

Still half-packed in my mind.

Still doing bedtime like a pro and still crying where no one can hear it.

But under all that, something new is muttering:

A tired, pissed-off little voice saying:

Maybe it's not that you were never worth staying for.

Maybe it's that none of them ever knew how to stay.

For once, I don't argue with it.

I lean back on that ugly couch, listen to my kids breathing down the hall, and think:

This isn't done yet.

And maybe — quietly, stubbornly, against all logic — that's where healing actually starts

CHAPTER SIXTEEN

The Bar Prophet

***

By late summer, I was still learning how fast life can pivot in one night.

The first weekend Jeff took the kids, the house didn't feel peaceful. It felt exposed.
I didn't have the tools yet to rest in quiet.

My brain treated silence like a warning.
Jeff finally started taking the kids, and I haven't had space since he left

It should've felt like relief.

It did, at first.

Two nights when I wasn't "Mom" on duty every second, where the house wasn't a command center, where I could finally hear myself think.

I had time.

And if you've never had real time — quiet time— your brain doesn't automatically do something healthy with it.

It panics.

Quiet time sounds like a reward to people who grew up with it. To me, it sounded like the moment right before a door slams. I'd sit there and feel my shoulders climb toward my ears, my hands restless, my brain scanning for the next hit.
No one was yelling. No one was coming.
But my body didn't believe that yet.

So instead of resting, I went looking for noise —
because noise at least felt familiar.

I started getting out.

Which was a big mistake.

One night I went to the local bar.

And yes, I already know. We all know.

Bar hookups are a disaster.

But you're talking about someone who hadn't been
out much — let alone someone whose brain had been in
a blender.

That kind of brain is easy to smooth talk.

That kind of brain doesn't hear red flags.

It hears attention.

It hears, "You're not invisible."

It hears, "Come sit by me."

And there is something about being seen after
you've been surviving that makes you stupid on a
cellular level.

If there was ever a time I could erase part of my
life, this would be it.

I was already broken down. I was already running
on fumes. I didn't need romance.

I needed help.

Who admits that?

But when you're me — when your operating system
is ***be useful, be quiet, don't need too much***—getting
help never helps.

So you accept the counterfeit version of it.

You accept the guy with the story.

And I met one.

A real piece of shit.

I don't say that because I'm mad, he didn't call.

I say that because this is the man who doesn't just disappoint you.

He reprograms you.

He came in with a great story.

He owned his own business. (Lie.)

He was going through what he called a toxic relationship with his kids 'mom. (Translation: there was a woman somewhere who had receipts.)

He was living with a friend "just temporarily." (Translation; grown man, permanent excuses.)

He helped his buddy out at the bar on weekends. (Translation: he had the perfect cover for why he was always there, always charming, always "misunderstood.")

And the bar backed him up without even trying.

Everybody knew him.

Everybody liked him (tolerated him)

Everybody had that same tone when they talked about him — like he was one of those "good guys" who just got dealt a bad hand.

My dumb brain did what it always did back then:

It took the crowd's opinion as character evidence.

I watched people approach him — laughing, hugging, slapping his back like he was family.

I watched women smile at him like he was harmless.

I watched men talk about how "strong" he was.

I remember thinking the most dangerous thought on earth:

If everyone likes him, he must be safe.

That's how you can tell I haven't healed yet.

Healed people don't confuse popularity with integrity.

But me?

I was still the foster kid in a grown woman body, reading rooms like survival.

If the room seemed calm, I assumed the person was safe.

I didn't realize you can be the most dangerous thing in the building and still be the most liked.

And then there was the warning.

Just one.

One older man — out of fifty-plus people — walked up to me and said, plain as day:

"Be careful. He's an asshole."

No flirting. No performance. No drama.

Just a warning delivered like a man who'd seen a pattern and was tired of watching women step into it.

That should've been my exit.

That should've been when I grabbed my purse and went home and bragged later like, "See? I finally listened to my gut."

But my gut was still in rehab.

And being me, I chuckled it off like it was disgruntled gossip.

Like the guy was just cranky.

He probably didn't like him because he was jealous.

I should've listened.

What an idiot I was.

Because warnings don't come with:

A soundtrack.

They don't come with dramatic lighting.

They come with a calm sentence you ignore.

And you've already picked the story you already imagined in your head.

And I had already picked.

The idea of choosing me — even for a night — made me feel something.

That's how low my bar was.

Not "is he kind?"

Not "is he stable?"

Not "does he treat women like humans?"

Just:

He sees me.

And if you've ever been lonely in the specific way that comes from being a single mom with too much trauma and not enough sleep, you know how "being seen" can feel like oxygen.

And yes, I ignored the warning and leaned into the lie.

He talked to me like he knew me.

Like I wasn't "a lot."

Like my brain was charming.

Like my story didn't scare him.

And that's one of the oldest tricks there is: acting like he can handle a woman's pain so she hands him access.

To be clear,

I wasn't falling for a man.

I was falling for the role he was auditioning for.

The "rescuer."
The "good guy."
The "everyone loves me so I must be safe" guy.

I was exactly the type of woman that act works on — because I wasn't looking for fireworks. I already had that along with a hidden nuclear bomb.

I was looking for a break.

I was looking for someone to walk into my life and not add weight to it.

I was looking for a minute where I didn't feel like a single human holding up an entire collapsing world.

So, when he came in smooth and confident, I didn't question it.

I let it in.

I hate admitting that part

Because I wasn't clueless.

My chest tightened with recognition. I was trained.

I recognized the blend of charm and threat like it was a familiar perfume.

And of course, they say you date someone like your father.

I used to hate that saying.

It sounded like blame.

Like it was telling me, "You're stupid. And it's your fault."

But the truth is, it isn't about stupidity.

It's about familiarity.

Your body recognizes what it grew up around.

And when life like I lived in feels normal, peace can feel suspicious.

That being said, when a man shows up with that exact cocktail — big story, bigger excuses, someone else to blame — my brain doesn't scream.

My brain relaxes.

Because it knows the language.

That's what makes it so sick.

That's what I didn't see that night.

I didn't see what he was.

I saw what I needed him to be.

I saw a person-shaped pause button.

The bar did the rest — noise, lights, laughter — like a fog machine over the truth.

So yes.

Jeff started taking the kids on weekends.

I started trying to breathe again.

I picked the worst possible place to practice being alive.

Because some men don't walk into your life as a lesson.

They walk in like a slow leak.

At first it's nothing.

Then it's damage.

Then one day you look around and realize you've been living in the aftermath for a long time.

You don't even remember the exact moment you stopped being free.

That's how the "savior" showed up — already holding out his hand for payment.

Because the next part is where the "great story" stops being a story.

Starts becoming a pattern.

One I didn't recognize fast enough.

One I stayed in way longer than any woman with a functioning head on her shoulders would've

Yes — before you ask — I know.

I know.

I was blind on purpose.

I was doing it with instinct, not awareness.

But he did see it—my need, my exhaustion, my soft spots—and he priced them.

CHAPTER SEVENTEEN

The Savior Discount

***

$\mathcal{T}$he following year, I learned what it costs when someone sells themselves as your savior.

I was packing my life into boxes. And he asked what I needed.

I told him the truth.

I'd had to move because of my divorce. And there was no one who could help me

We moved to this town not knowing anyone and I was left here alone with my kids not knowing anyone.

Just me, a life collapsing into boxes, and that familiar feeling of being the one who has to figure it out.

He nodded like he understood.

Then he did something that — at the time — felt like God finally throwing me a bone.

He got ahold of his cousin.

He rounded up help.

He made calls. He showed up. He had bodies. He had muscle. He had a plan.

And because I was me, because I'd spent my whole life being the one who handled everything alone, I mistook basic effort for a miracle.

He was living with his friend then. Didn't have a place for his kids to stay with him.

I was moving into a new place with three bedrooms.

So the logic seemed clean:

When his kids come over, mine can share a room.
Everybody fits.
Everybody wins.
We're building something.

He looked like the solution to all my problems.

Not in a dramatic fairytale way.

In the way that gets single moms hooked:

He shows up on time.

Doesn't ask questions.

Help that makes you feel like you're not drowning
for one whole day.

We move things into storage.
He helped me into the new place.
Then, cleaned the house I was losing.

Right after the dust settled — right after he'd played
hero — he asked me for money.

$750.00.

You know what that should've been?

My first clue.

That moment should of opened my eyes.

Wait. Why does the savior have an invoice?

But he had an excuse ready. And it slid right into
my soft spot like it was made for it:

His cousin needed to be paid.
The buddies who helped him move needed paid.
He didn't want to look bad.
He needed it right away.

I understood and paid it.

Because I'm smart in a courtroom and dumb in a
kitchen.

Because I can argue property codes to a county commissioner and still get conned by a man with a sad face and a believable sentence.

Later I found out it was a lie.

But at the time?

Everything looked like it was panning out.

And that's the dangerous part.

The beginning didn't feel like a trap.

It felt like momentum.

I was busting my ass healing — top- notch.

I was back in school.

I bought a big deep freeze and filled it with meat from a butcher like I was finally doing that "stable family" thing for real.

I was working two jobs.

He was helping with the kids — being there when they got out of school.

He'd allow me to sleep while he watched them.

And if you've ever been a mom so tired you start forgetting words mid-sentence, you know how seductive that is.

Sleep is not rest.

Sleep is survival.

So in my mind, I built the story:

This is good.

This is different.

This is what it looks like when someone shows up.

I paid all the bills — because I wasn't depending on a man to pay them.

He would "give what he could," because child support was leaving him almost broke.

That sounded responsible.

That sounded like a man trying.

And I wanted to believe it so badly I could've framed it and hung it up next to my freezer.

Then one night I went to get dinner out, and when I came back from the garage, I noticed there was a lot of food missing.

Not "we've been eating well" missing.

Missing like someone had taken advantage of the fact I couldn't keep an inventory in my head because I was running on stress and fumes.

At first I assumed the easiest explanation:

Someone's getting into the garage.

And he put that idea in my head too — like he was helping.

"Yeah, babe, someone probably is getting in the garage at night."

So, I did what a normal person do when they thought someone was stealing.

I put a padlock on the freezer.

Problem solved.

Except... it wasn't.

Because the supply kept going down anyway.

Which is a special kind of mindfuck because you start questioning your own reality.

Did I imagine it?

Did I count wrong?

Am I losing it?

That's how it starts.

Not with a punch.

With you doubting your own eyes.

Then I started noticing other things.

Little shifts.

Little scenes.

Like there were young girls hanging out in our garage with him and his buddy.

Girls who lived down the road.

Girls who were too comfortable.

Girls who weren't there for "a quick hello."

And I heard them talking — casually, like it was normal — about the steaks he'd been bringing them.

About how fresh they were.

That's when the pieces started lining up.

Not in a dramatic way.

In a quiet, nauseating way.

The realization that makes your stomach go cold because you can feel your life pivoting without your permission.

Then I went to my storage unit.

And the lock was changed.

Not "someone tried to break in."

Changed.

Things were missing.

I stood there staring at my own unit like it was a stranger's, trying to make my brain accept what my body already knew:

This isn't random.

This is inside my house.

This is in my life.

My son started saying things that made me want to crawl out of my skin.

He told me Glenn was spending a lot of time with those girls.

My stomach dropped so hard it felt like my body missed a step.
My ears started ringing—like my brain was trying to shut the sentence off before it could land.

I didn't need anyone to connect the dots for me.
They weren't "women."
They were girls.

Seventeen. Nineteen. Twenty-one, I think.
His buddy's daughters.

And somehow, because I was still living in my own version of denial with a pretty bow on it, he talked me into letting them babysit when I needed a sitter.
He framed it like he was doing me a favor. Like it was harmless.
And if I hesitated, he made me feel like I was being uptight for even questioning it.

I didn't have the full picture yet. He liked it that way.
Those girls liked pills.
And Glenn liked the attention it brought.

Glenn knew about Sarah's prescription pills.
And that gave Glenn control—the kind he liked.

I wasn't built to recognize this kind of game.
My brain didn't come with the manual for this part of the hustle.

I wasn't thinking "drug dealer."
"Predator."

"Criminal behavior is now orbiting my children."

Because in my head, that life was a phase people grew out of.
Young and dumb.
A bad era.
Something that happened to other people.
Not me.
Not my lifestyle.
I wasn't raised in that world. I wasn't street-smart in that way.
I thought that part of life was long gone—outdated.
I thought I'd already paid my dues in hell.

Turns out, hell doesn't care what you think you've graduated from.
It just changes costumes from a clean-cut professional to complete gutter garbage with fancy manipulation.
And this one walked into my house carrying a moving box and a sob story... and left fingerprints on everything I owned.
I did not realize yet he was not just stealing from me. He was building an audience with my hard-earned money
Because once you see the lock changed, and the cupboards empty, and the girls too comfortable in your garage...
you're not in a relationship anymore.
You're in a situation.
Situations don't end politely.

CHAPTER EIGHTEEN

Town of Witnesses

***

A year later, I lived in a town full of witnesses—

and still had to prove I was bleeding.

I learned the worst part isn't the danger, it's the audience.

It was one of those stretches when we were trying to live normal in the same small town that never forgets your name.

It started with meat missing.

Then it turned into something worse.
Food wasn't just food. It was showing that I was trying. That I was building something stable out of scraps. That I could still be a mom who planned ahead instead of a mom who survived minute to minute.

So when things kept disappearing, I told myself the lie that felt safest:

And then the universe — being the universe — said," That's cute."

Because the next thing that started going missing wasn't food

It was pills.

The kind you don't "misplace."

You don't shrug off.

You notice because your whole day is built around them.

At first I did what I always do when reality gets too ugly:

I tried to make it make sense without making it real.

Maybe I counted wrong.

Maybe I put the bottle somewhere else.

Maybe the pharmacy shorted it.

Maybe I'm just tired.

Because, if I admitted what my gut was screaming, then I'd have to admit I'd let a threat live inside my house with my kids.

I wasn't ready to feel that kind of shame yet.

That's one of the worst parts of survival: you don't just get hurt.

You also get embarrassed.

He started doing these late-night "runs."

Always with his buddy down the road.

Always casual.

Always "back in a minute."

And if you asked questions, you weren't being careful — you were being crazy.

That was his favorite trick.

Not explaining or reassuring. Just making *you* feel stupid for even wondering.

Meanwhile, I started noticing things that made my stomach drop:

Kids left overnight with no one home.

Not once.

More than once.

I didn't have the luxury of disbelief, and it showed. That's when fear turned into action, my kids weren't going to be anybody's leverage to control me.

The thing you don't even process at first because it's so reckless your brain rejects it.

You walk into a room thinking,

Okay, good, they're being watched.

And then you realize the house is too quiet.

No adult noise.

TV off.

No footsteps.

Just kids — alone — because the adults decided they had better things to do.

The second I realized that, something in me went dead calm.

Not calm like peaceful.

Calm like a switch flipped.

The part of me that negotiates. Gone.

The excuses I make to try to keep the story pretty. Gone.

All that was left was the mother part that doesn't care how charming you are.

If you endanger my kids, you're not a boyfriend anymore.

You're a problem.

And problems don't get cuddled.

I confronted him.

It went exactly the way it always goes when you confront a man who lives off other people's confusion.

First: denial.

Then: blame.

Then: anger.

The moment he realized I wasn't buying it anymore, the mask slipped.

Not dramatically.

Not like a movie.

Like a door that finally stops latching.

He started pushing me around.

Dragging me on the floor.

Telling me he would kill me if I left him.

Saying it like it was normal.

Like it was something you say to a woman the way you say "goodnight."

And in that moment, I didn't feel romantic heartbreak.

I felt disgusted

It's not love.

It's ownership.

I was done being owned.

So I threw him out.

Not politely.

Not with closure.

Not with some emotional speech where he suddenly understands and cries and changes.

I threw him out the way you throw out something rotten before it poisons the whole house.

He left real easy, which was odd.

Later I realized why—he already had somewhere to go.

He packed his clothes and walked to his buddy's
down the road with the young girls.
And he stayed there until he got his own place.
I remember feeling relieved. I thought he'd found
someone else to fixate on. Which I found out later

he was involved with the oldest daughter.
I thought that meant I was free.
Which would've been impressive if he'd actually
had money.
But he did have money.
He had access to my stuff

I learned the hard way that some men don't "get
back on their feet."
They stand on yours.

After he left, the truth didn't come all at once.
It came in pieces.

And he didn't stop trying to control me just because
he changed addresses.
From that house, he still threatened me—still made
it hard for me to go to work, still made it hard for
anyone else to watch my kids.
Like the distance meant nothing.
Like he still had a hand on the wheel.

Levi, eleven maybe twelve at the time, is the one
who seen something he should have never seen,

something that confirmed what my gut had been trying to scream at me for months.

I'm not going to dress that up.

It made me sick.

It made me furious in some sense but relieved in another

It made me want to rewind my life and physically drag my own past self out of that bar by her ponytail.

Because this wasn't just "bad boyfriend behavior."

This was predatory.

He was dangerous.

This was a man who not only breaks your heart.

He also, breaks the rules.

Rules of what you thought was possible around your children.

And then there were the rumors.

Rumors about their dad. About what he'd done to them.

They denied all of it. So I told myself it was just that — rumors.

Because I wanted to believe the best in a situation that didn't deserve it.

It was hard believing the worst because it meant admitting how close my kids had been to a kind of harm I don't even like naming.

Later, I found out different.

And the part that still turns my stomach?

Sarah's pills were currency.

Her medication was paying for things that should never be bought with a child's stability.

My food was paying their way.

My freezer was funding lies, late nights, favors and secrets.

The "money" he'd show up with — just enough to keep me thinking he was trying?

It wasn't demonstrating responsibility.

It was evident that he'd sold something of mine.

That's what useless men of his standards do.

They don't earn.

They convert your life into cash.

Piece by piece.

You'd think after I threw him out, it would end.

But men like that don't leave like normal men.

They don't just disappear.

They retaliate after the fixation that made them feel untouchable was gone.

After he left my house, he started threatening me.

He threatened to burn my vehicle down — with me and the kids in it.

He would have friends slam me in public, yelling things at me like I wasn't a person, like I was something they could shout at for sport.

They screamed, "daddy fucker" like they knew my history, like they were proud to weaponize it, like my trauma was town's property.

And the worst part?

It worked.

Because the it felt like the whole town was on his side.

That's not me being dramatic.

That's the reality of small places and big mouths.

He had the charm.
He had the network.

He had the "poor guy" story.
He had the buddy system.
And I had what I always had:
Kids.
Bills.
Receipts.
And the reputation of being the woman who "causes problems" the second she refuses to be used.
If you've never been in that position, I'll explain what it feels like.
It feels like the whole world becomes a hallway.
You can hear people talking before you even turn the corner.
It feels like everyone knows your business, but not your truth.
It feels like being punished for surviving out loud.
That messed with my head in a way that took years to undo — because when you're already pre-programmed to blame yourself, public humiliation doesn't feel like an attack.
It feels like confirmation.
Like the universe going, "See? Told you."
But, here's what I didn't understand yet:
When a whole town sides with a man like that, it's not because he's right.
It's because he's useful.
It's because they fear if they don't what would he say or do to them.

He's the town's entertainment. He's familiar.

I was the woman who disrupted the vibe by refusing to be quiet and reaching out for help.

Just to be turned away with no responses and looking like I was crazy.

That's something people don't get.
They think leaving is one moment.
One decision.
One brave speech.
Sometimes leaving is a season.
It can be a war.
Sometimes it's you locking your doors, checking the windows, watching the driveway, and still getting up the next day to make breakfast like your life isn't being hunted.
I did all of that with one thought stuck in my throat:
I picked him
I let him into my life.
I handed him access because he moved boxes and told a good story.
I should've listened to that older man in the bar.
I should've listened to my gut.
I should've—
But "should've" is something that are wasted years in woman like me.
So instead of drowning in it, I did the only thing knew when life turns into hell:
I went into action.
Not dramatic kind.
The boring kind.

Documentation.

Dates.

Names.

Patterns.

For once, my survival mode worked in my favor.

Because, if I learned anything from my life, it's this:

If you don't write it down, they rewrite it for you.

I wasn't letting him rewrite this.

Not with my kids in the story.

Not with my name on the line.

Not again.

And right about then, the outside world showed up with its favorite advice: "Just leave."

Because this is the point where it stops being "I dated the wrong man." And becomes:

How do you survive a man who doesn't accept being removed from your life?

CHAPTER NINETEEN

"Just Leave"

***

By mid-summer, "just leave" became the stupidest advice anyone could say out loud.

Here's what I learned: leaving isn't one decision. It's a thousand small moves, and every one of them costs something.

This was the season when leaving wasn't one big moment — it was kids, logistics, and a whole town watching like it was entertainment.

I'm not a perfect person.

The choices I've made can be judged,

ridiculed, and painted like I'm just ignorant — like I'm some idiot who "can't just leave."

How many times have you heard someone say it?

"Just leave him."

"I don't understand why you keep yourself in this position."

"It's easy to get out, you pay your own bills."

It does sound easy when it flows out of someone's mouth.

It's a neat sentence. A clean little solution. One of those phrases people throw out like they're handing you a life jacket.

But if you've ever been the person inside the situation, the person actually living it — you know that sentence doesn't come with the things you need to make it real.

It doesn't come with childcare.

And the little, humiliating logistics nobody talks about:

A security deposit you don't have

A phone that won't get shut off mid-plan

A ride, a tank of gas, and a place that won't ask questions

A school pickup plan that doesn't expose where you're sleeping

A court system that moves fast enough to matter

A town that won't call you "dramatic" for trying to stay alive

It doesn't come with a safe place to go, someone to help you move, a witness, protection, or a place that believes you.

When you have small kids and not a single person on your side, "just leave" isn't a sentence.

It's a fantasy.

Because, leaving isn't just walking out a door.

Leaving is getting your life back from someone who believes they own it.

As time went on, the man I was trying to leave didn't calm down.

He got stronger.

Not physically. Strategically.

He was collecting knowledge about me like it was ammunition.

He called my dad — the man that destroyed me in the beginning and throughout

He called my mother — the one who tried to kill me every chance she got and knew nothing about me

And he got every angle he could with information that was not valid but usable

He went around telling *their* stories like they were his.

My mom's "daddy's rape child" became "daddy fucker."

It wasn't rumors anymore.

He got "confirmation" from my own mother and was using it.

My dad's story got spun into:

I destroyed my marriage.
He had to save my ex-husband from me.

He built a version of me that was so ugly, so twisted, so easy to hate... that people didn't have to feel uncomfortable supporting him.

That's what smear campaigns are all about

They don't have to prove you're the villain.

They have to make it believable enough that no one questions it.

I had no one.

I was isolated.

Every move controlled.

People don't factor in when they say "just leave."

They picture a breakup.

What I was in wasn't a breakup.

It was containment.

There were times he would walk into my house and I wanted him to leave.

So I did what people always say you should do.
I called the cops.
Even the cops would stand there and bullshit with him like they were old friends.
Because they were.
He went to school with them.
So while I'm standing there, terrified, trying to get a grown man out of my house. The people who are meant to protect you are joking with him like he's the homecoming king who just got a little too loud.
Then they'd make comments to him, like they were on his side.
Like I was the inconvenience.
Like I was the dramatic woman they had to "manage."
That's another thing people don't understand.
When the system doesn't take you seriously, it teaches the predator that he can do whatever he wants.
It trains him.
It emboldens him.
It tells him:
You're safe.
She's not.
Keep going.

I got PPO's
The PPOs still weren't enforced.
On paper, I had protection.
In real life, I had paperwork.
Paper doesn't stop a man who's already decided you're his.

Paper doesn't stop a man when the people enforcing it don't feel like enforcing it.

So I was trapped in the most insulting kind of situation:

I couldn't leave my own home without getting shamed, harassed, and cornered by his friends.

I couldn't stay without being stalked by him.

If I went out, there were eyes.

If I stayed in, there was fear.

The whole town felt like it belonged to him.

And I was just... living in it.

Like a target.

That's why "just leave" makes me laugh.

Because it's clueless.

Leaving isn't easy when the punishment follows you.

Leaving isn't easy when the town becomes his weapon.

Leaving isn't easy when the police treat him like a buddy and treat you like a nuisance.

Leaving isn't easy when you're raising kids and trying to keep them calm while your own body is living in constant adrenaline.

And yes — my kids were with me through this whole thing, and he played like there was nothing wrong in front of them, he knew I wouldn't do anything while they were there

People just love to judge the hardest.

Like I was naive

Like I didn't care.

Like I wasn't trying every day to keep them fed, safe, medicated, stable, and unaware of how much danger was orbiting our life.

Meanwhile, their dad?

He was drinking.

Living life without worry.

Existing in his own world while mine was a rotating emergency.

I didn't have the luxury of falling apart.

I had to keep moving.

Even while I was scared.

 I was ashamed.

 I was watching the people who should've helped me act like I was exaggerating.

Eventually, I did what people keep saying you should do.

I attempted to leave.

Not physically because that was already done.

Leaving emotionally.

I left because I couldn't keep my life standing while he kept kicking the legs out from under it.

Because of it he started calling my jobs.

Telling them I was on drugs.

Making up lies that sounded "concerned" to people who didn't know him.

And my body was already dealing with new damage after chemo.

I'd started having seizures.

I had one at the AFC home I was working at.

An ambulance showed up.

At the hospital they ran a full drug panel—everything.
Negative. Of course it was negative.

But the lie didn't die just because the test came back
clean.
About a month passed and I kept getting drug tested. I
quit because the house manager believed him.

I found another job. I liked working with the youth.
But I couldn't afford that little house anymore—too
many jobs lost, too much instability, and then the issue
with my daughter's service dog on top of it.
So I did what I had to do.
I took the income-based apartment because it was what
I could get.

That's where it got bad.
He realized I was moving to his neck of the woods.

Because when you leave a controlling man and you
enter his territory, he doesn't back off.
He escalates.
This isn't the end.
It's the trigger.

The apartment wasn't freedom.
It was his next stage.
It was the moment he couldn't control me inside my
house ... he could control me outside of it.

No one warns you.
That's the part "just leave" doesn't cover.

So, if you're reading this thinking, "Why didn't she
leave sooner?"
Here's the real answer:
I did leave.
Over and over

In pieces.

In steps.

In survival decisions.

Every time I tried, he adjusted.

He learned.

He got louder.

He got smarter.

He got help.

All I had was... me.

Me, two kids, and a system that kept handing him confidence and handing me paperwork.

So, we moved into the apartment, and the door stopped meaning anything.

Because that's where the story stops being about a bad choice at a bar...

and becomes about what happens when a man decides your life is his entertainment.

And he was just getting warmed up.

The apartment smelled like cheap carpet and dingy old odors.

I was starting to get used to my apartment life and the kids were excelling in school, when my phone started up again.

And that's when I realized moving in his territory just relocated the playing field.

CHAPTER TWENTY

Exhibit A

***

By the end of that year, I had moved—but the battlefield followed.

There are moments where you didn't need another lesson.

You need to show you were not imagining the old one.

For me, it didn't look like justice.

It looked like paperwork.

A folder.

A stack of dates.

A list of calls that went nowhere.

A name was written down because I knew the story would get rewritten if I didn't.

That's what people don't understand when they say, "Just call the cops."

They talk about the system like it is a door you walk through.

It's supposed to give that vibe "If you just say the words, everything just disappears." Maybe in my old life but I don't want what comes with that life.

The system is not a door.

It is a mirror.

And if you are not believed, or it requires too much effort, you don't get protection

By the time Glenn came into my life, my body already knew how this works.

Not from books or articles

But flashbacks of how my dad could walk away no matter what he did to people. He was untouchable for a long time.

When things started getting ugly my brain did what it usually does in events like this

It went looking for recaps

I found two newspaper clippings from the eighties.

Same county energy.

Same kind of man.

Same kind of outcome.

Those clippings were not strangers to me. It was my dad kidnapping and beating my mom in a car two days after he got released from jail for beating her with a table leg.

That man in the headline was my father.

That woman was my mother.

And I was thirteen — watching a system look straight at violence and still leave the door unlocked.

That is the first time I learned the difference between charges and consequences.

Paper can say protection.

But paper cannot stand between you and a man who already learned the rules don't stop him.

So, when Glenn started circling my life like he had rights to it, my body didn't call it "new."
It called it familiar.
Because I had already watched what happens when a violent man gets treated like a temporary inconvenience instead of a threat.

Two hours later after getting released, he kidnaps her and beats her again.
Two hours.

That is not a mistake.
That is what happens when you hand a violent man the message that consequences are negotiable.

The article described the injuries in a way that made my stomach go cold.
Broken nose.
Face gouged up.
Head slammed into a dashboard.
A woman trying to jump out of a moving car because that felt safer than staying inside it.

And the part that hit me the hardest was not even the violence.
It was the pattern on both their parts.

Because right there, in black and white, was the
same trap I have watched women fall into over and over
After the assault, she wanted to drop the charges.

Hmm, I think about when she left me in that house
alone when he went to jail the first time and he found
out about it when he got out.

People love to act like she lied. She didn't.
Or she forgave him. There was more to that.
Or she was just "dramatic."
Or was she holding a secret that made her feel
guilty herself and she dropped the charges?

Those of us who have lived it know the truth.
Dropping charges is not always forgiveness.
Sometimes it is a hostage negotiation.

When the system does not protect you, you start
trying to manage the danger yourself.
You start making choices based on what will keep
you alive this week.
Not what will look brave on paper.

Then I read the second clipping.
Months later.
Same case.

The headline might as well have said, "Here is how
the system finishes what he started."
Prosecution drops the kidnapping charge.

Not because the story was not violent.
Not because the injuries were not real.

Because the defense attacked her credibility.

That is the oldest move in the book.
If you cannot defend what he did, you put her on
trial instead.

A witness says she looked fine.
Another says she was emotional.
Somebody repeats the same poison women have
been hearing forever:
She is lying.
She is unstable.
She is doing it for attention.

And then the violence gets negotiated down until it
fits inside a smaller box.
A deal.
A misdemeanor.
Time served.

Do you know what that teaches a man like that?
It teaches him that the ceiling is higher than he
thought.
That the system will bargain with the wrong person.

It teaches him he can push harder next time.

That is the part nobody wants to say out loud.
When the system fails softly, it trains predators.

Bond.
Time served.
Dropped charges.
"Domestic." "Civil." "Nothing we can do unless..."

Small permissions.
Big consequences.

I sat there holding those clippings and realized why
Glenn acted the way he did.
 The boldness.
The entitlement.
The confidence that he could show up, push
boundaries, and still be treated like the reasonable one.

Because the system does not just fail women,
it educates men like him.

It teaches them what they can get away with.
How far they can go before anyone stops them.

So, when I tried to get help and got treated like I
was the problem, I was not surprised.
I was sick.
Because I have seen this script before.

And once a man realizes the consequences are
optional, he stops asking for permission.

He starts acting like the door is already open.

That is how you end up living in a place where "leave" is not a moment.
It is a strategy.
A schedule.
A safety plan built around the fact that the system might show up, but it might not enforce anything.

So, I kept documenting.
I knew it wasn't going to save me.
But I did know what happens if I didn't have it.
The story gets rewritten without you.

And Glenn was counting on that.
That is how an open-door policy gets written.

CHAPTER TWENTY-ONE

Open-Door Policy

***

*B*y the time he started walking into my apartment like he owned oxygen, I already knew the system wasn't going to save me.

He didn't "keep showing up."

He waltzed in.

Like my apartment had an open-door policy. Like my lease came with a bonus roommate who didn't pay rent but still acted like the couch provider.

He would just walk in and not leave.

I couldn't get him out the normal way.

Because the normal way requires a system that treats "get out of my home" like a sentence that matters.

The normal way requires cops who don't laugh.

The normal way requires enforcement.

What I had was this:

If I pushed too hard, he would get violent in front of my kids.

So, I learned a new survival skill:

I had to play the part.

Calm voice. Neutral face. No sudden movements. No escalation.

It wasn't because I was "weak."

It was because my kids were watching.

And he knew exactly how I would behave when they were around.

He knew I wouldn't escape in front of them.
He knew I wouldn't fight in front of them.
He knew I did take risks with them around.

He used my motherhood like it was a restraint system.

I need to put this out there because people picture monsters like they're stupid.

Glenn made sure he didn't treat me "that way" in front of my kids.

It wasn't because he had morals — he had a brain.

My kids would've been the best witnesses to his behavior. And he wasn't about to hand me witnesses. He wasn't about to hand me proof that couldn't be spun into "she's dramatic" or "she's exaggerating."

So, he ran two versions of himself:

Public Glenn: calm, friendly, reasonable, the guy everyone knows

Private Glenn: control, threats, violence, punishment — then the switch flips back like nothing happened

He didn't only control me.

He worked my kids too.

He'd say things to my son who was fifteen at the time — little lies, little seeds — trying to pull him into the "your mom is crazy" story so I stayed in line. Because if your own kid doubts you, you stop fighting as hard You start proving you're stable instead of protecting yourself.

He spoiled Sarah too. And I didn't understand why at first.

Later I did.

It wasn't love.

It was leverage.

Because I couldn't escape if he could mold my kids to hate me for trying.

I kept working.

Kept trying to pick myself up.

Kept doing the mom routine like I wasn't living inside a hostage situation with a welcome mat. This went on for about a year.

A year of him wandering around like he owned the place.

A year of me making calls.

A year of cops showing up and acting like I was entertainment

Like I was the joke.

Like I was the crazy one and he was the calm one.

Which is the oldest trick in the book:

Let the woman sound desperate.

Let the man sound reasonable.

Call it "a domestic."

Leave.

Every time they didn't remove him, it taught him something.

It taught him my "no" didn't count.

It taught him my home wasn't mine.

Then one day, I got a state trooper.

One call.

One person who didn't act like it was funny.

One person looked at the situation and treated it like what it was.

That was the day he got removed.

The world didn't suddenly became fair.

It was in the middle of trying to survive, I snapped.

I took my daughter's keyboard and hit him on the head.

Not a proud moment.

Not a "girl power" moment.

A fear moment.

A "get off me, get out, stop" moment.

After he was finally gone, it didn't turn into peace.

It turned into consequences.

My vehicle got keyed.

I got flat tires.

My kids got picked on at school.

I could take the hits, but I couldn't take my kids getting punished for something they didn't cause.

The message underneath all of it was loud and clear:

We can't get to you directly right now. So we'll punish everything around you.

I quit college again.

Because it's hard to focus on homework when you're checking your tires like a crime scene every morning.

It's hard to study when your kids are being targeted and you're trying to keep them stable.

It's hard to build a future when someone is committed to dragging you backward.

Briefly, I had help.

Not the fake kind.

Real help.

There was an older gentleman who was helping me.
He wasn't from that town.

He didn't come with the gossip and the "everybody knows" culture.

He was married, and his wife was amazing.

A woman you can tell is safe just by the way she looks you in the eye.

They took me to lunch.

Put me under their wing.

Not in a creepy way.

In a "you've been alone too long" way.

In a "we're going to help you make better choices because you deserve better choices" way.

And for one minute I could think clearly and my mind calmed down.

Because when you've been isolated kindness hits like confusion at first.

You keep waiting for something

One night they called, his wife was going to meet us after work. But he came and picked me up.

Here's where my fear showed up — because fear was always my most consistent companion.

Glenn didn't work at the bar anymore, but I was still terrified because it was his friend's bar.

I asked if there was somewhere else we could go.

Somewhere neutral.

Somewhere not connected to the people who treated my trauma like local entertainment.

But they insisted.

They said we needed to face it.

They said they would be there with me.

They said I would be safe.

And I believed them.

Because I wanted to believe that support meant protection.

So I went.

I showed up with the older gentleman.

Instantly Glenn came blasting out.

No build-up. No warning. No "talk."

He started punching the old man.

Just like that.

When he was done, he grabbed me and threw me into a vehicle.

He drove me back to the apartment and dragged me in.

He sat on top of me beating my head into the floor.

Over and over

He put an indent in my skull that's still there to this day.

Then I did the thing I hate admitting. But it's the truth:

I calmed him down.

Because survival will make you do things that don't look noble.

You learn to read breathing.

You learn to adjust your tone.

You learn the exact amount of compliance it takes to keep someone from going further.

That isn't love.

That's a hostage skill.

When he finally softened enough for me to move, I found my phone and called 911.

He grabbed it, removed the battery. And I escaped
to my car and drove toward the hospital.

And he chased me.

My chest was burning.

The steering wheel was slick in my hands.

I kept checking my mirror like if I looked hard enough,
I could make him disappear.

For one stupid second, the radio was still playing
like the world hadn't noticed I was fighting for my life.

Then because my life enjoys cruel plot twists, I got
pulled over.

Not him.

Me.

Because he was already on the phone with the cops
saying I was driving reckless and drunk.

I didn't drink.

But that didn't matter.

I got pulled out.

Given a sobriety test.

Treated like a criminal.

All while Glenn stood there acting like a hero —
pleading like he was just trying to save my life, like he
feared for my safety, like he was the responsible one.

And I tried to explain.

I tried.

But by then, the local cop already had a story in his
head:

That I was crazy.

That's the story Glenn had been painting for
months.

Once a man convinces the system you're unstable, everything you say sounds like he's right.

You don't sound like a victim.

You sound like "a problem."

So there I was — hurt, terrified, trying to get medical help — and I'm the one in the spotlight.

Me doing tests on the side of the road.

Me being judged.

Me being treated like the danger.

While the actual danger is standing there, calm, clean, and convincing.

That's how he did it.

He didn't hurt me.

He controlled the narrative of me.

And when you control the narrative, you control the response.

You control who gets believed.

You control who gets protected.

That's when I learned a phone number can be a weapon if you keep answering it.

Because after the apartment, after the bar, after the floor, after the chase...

This is where I stopped thinking I was just trying to "get away from a bad relationship."

I started realizing I was trying to survive a man who could weaponize an entire town.

CHAPTER TWENTY-TWO

The Number I Should've Blocked Forever

***

The first real quiet I'd had in months lasted exactly long enough for me to forget what peace cost, until my phone rang.

He disappeared for a minute.

Not the satisfying kind of disappearance where the universe finally admits you've suffered enough and hands you peace like an apology.

Just... gone.

One of his buddies was leaving out of town and offered him a house to sit and another daughter came of age.

Glenn was on top of the world.

Which was great.

Gone at last, I thought.

I remember the feeling—light, stupid, hopeful—like my body didn't know what to do without the constant threat hovering in the background.

I stood there in my kitchen and let myself believe, for one breath, this was done.

I should've treated that quiet like a gift.

I should've protected it with my life.

Instead, I answered a phone call.

It was a number I wasn't familiar with.

And my first mistake was doing what I always did back then: assuming there was a normal explanation.

He said he was calling for his mom.
He needed help with unemployment because she got fired from a job she'd worked for twenty-five years.
Twenty-five.
Just saying that makes you angry.
The problem was... I loved his mom.
I genuinely did.
She was a victim of his evil too, whether she admitted it out loud or not.
So my guard dropped—just enough.

Because she was there, I didn't feel threatened.
Because I'd heard he'd "moved on," my brain let itself believe the danger had taken its show on the road.
Because I wanted to be the person who helps people, I went.
That's what still gets me.

I didn't walk into that house thinking, I'm about to be hurt.
I walked into that house thinking, I'm about to help a woman who doesn't deserve this.
When I arrived, she was there.
Good.
She was real. She was present. She was breathing in front of me, not just a name used to lure me into a trap.
And Glenn had a friend there too, Jim
Safer yet, I thought.

Because my brain was still doing that old math:
Witness = safety.
Other adult present = limits.
Someone will step in if something happens.

That is what a sane person believes.
That is what a person should be allowed to believe.
I helped his mom.
We did what we needed to do.
And when she got up to leave, I did too—right behind her, because I wasn't there to socialize. I wasn't there to "catch up." I was there to do a task and get out.

But before I could follow her out the door, Glenn stopped me. He said the sentence that should've made my blood run cold:
"Jim needs help too, since you're here." Jim was still sitting there. I was unsure.
Jim was there, what could happen?
I was safe.
It was fine.
I can get through it.
And be out of there.
I still remember the smell in that kitchen—coffee and whatever cheap cleaner was used— the room was trying to convince me this was just a normal afternoon.

"And that's what predators look for:"
You do not want to be rude.
Not wanting conflict.

They count on the part of you that has survived so much that you'll do anything to keep the situation from escalating in front of someone.

He waited until his mom drove off.

At that moment.

I know it was intentional.

It wasn't "a misunderstanding" or "he snapped" or any other excuse people use to make evil sound accidental. The second her car was gone; he pulled me off the barstool by my hair.

Jim was right there.

Right there!

And he did nothing.

He sat there.

Glenn dragged me down the hall.

He hit me and threw me on the bed.

I remember my body going numb—like my brain was trying to shut off to protect itself, like I was slipping out of my own skin.

Then he raped me.

I'm not going to dress that up with softer words.

That's what it was.

While it was happening, I was screaming for help.

Jim was still there!

Doing nothing.

That part is almost as sickening as the assault itself—the knowledge that another human being can hear you begging and decide, nah she's not worth the inconvenience.

At some point I started coming to, and Glenn was out of the room already talking to Jim like they were discussing a chore.

Like it was the way it had to be.

Like he was teaching me a lesson.

I heard him say something about keeping a woman in line.

Like a dog.

He was claiming ownership of me like property.

And this was what men do.

I got dressed as fast as my hands moved.

Jim was walking out the door.

And something in me—pure panic, pure survival—went after him.

I ran out of the house screaming, "Don't leave. Please help me," chasing him to his car. If I could just get one decent person to turn around, my life could still make sense. He kept walking.

Jim got in his car, and I chased him down the driveway.

My feet slipped on gravel as the distance opened between us.

Glenn caught me mid-stride.

Fingers knotted in my hair, yanking hard enough to snap my head back.

My feet flew out from under me and I went down, dragged backward up the driveway, skin scraping, knees slamming, breath tearing out of my chest.

I tried to get my footing. Couldn't. My legs dangling, my body folding as his fist stayed twisted in my hair, pulling, jerking, keeping me off balance.

We crossed the porch. I tripped again.

He grabbed my arm and hauled me inside, dragging me across the floor into the living room. My shoulder hit first. Then my hip. Then my back.

He lifted me by the throat and slammed me into the beam.

The impact rattled through my spine. My head rang. White flashes came across my sight.

"I'm going to kill you," he said.

Not shouted.

Not rushed.

Said like a fact.

He let go just long enough to grab my hair again, shoved me down onto the couch, and pressed in with a pillow over my face—his weight crushing, a hand on my neck, cutting air.

The room narrowed. Sound thinned. My body stopped thinking in sentences.

This is where language drops out.

There was no plan. No thought. Just movement—scratching, shoving, bucking, grabbing for anything that might make him loosen his grip. Nails raking skin. Teeth clenched. Muscles firing without permission.

Animals fighting.

I got my hands free enough to do the only thing I could think of in that moment—go for anything that would make him let go. I dug my thumb into his jaw and ground back and forth penetrating through his skin, digging deeper and deeper—anything to make him let go. I couldn't see or breathe through that pillow. All I had was flashbacks.

My kids bursting through my head like strobe lights. Faces. Voices. Noise without words.

I pushed harder.

My thumb slid, caught, and dug back in. Wet. Slippery. I felt it before I saw it—blood starting to run.

He jerked.

He loosened up.

The second he did, I ran.

I got to my car.

And reaching for my gun and I stopped and thought of his kids.

I pulled my hands back out of the glove box angry at myself for being so weak.

My hands started shaking so hard, I hit my steering wheel with the loudest scream *"WHAT THE FUCK IS WRONG WITH YOU?"* I looked back and here he was running toward my car and tried to put my keys in the ignition. Dropped them. Snatched them up again, fingers slipping, metal clattering like it didn't want to cooperate.

Everything felt too small, my hands, the wheel, the space between seconds—as if even the car was trying to get away from what was coming.

For one second, my mind may have gone to the darkest thoughts of what I could do, fear does that. It makes you think in extremes.

Then another thought hit even harder:

I was already the "crazy one" in the eyes of the law.

That wasn't paranoia. That's experience.

I could already see the story being told about me, the way it always went:

She's unstable look at her past.

She's dramatic.

She's lying her whole family says it.

She's a murderer, her dad was.

He was just trying to calm her down.

So, I didn't choose the dramatic exit.

I chose the living exit.

I did what women like me learn to do when we're trying to survive men like him:

I lied.

I told him I had to go pick up Sarah from school.

I told him they'd been calling me.

I made false promises—whatever words would keep him from pulling me back into that house.

I said whatever would get me away.

And I left.

When I pulled onto the road, I realized I could still make choices—tiny ones, but mine.

I drove back to the apartment shaking so hard my hands didn't feel like mine.

When I got inside, I did the one thing people always say to do, like it fixes everything:

I called the cops.

And this is where my life started drowning in paperwork.

I gave them the facts.

I was reading my own wounds out loud.
The PPO was still active. No contact—period.
He'd used a blocked number, baited me with his mother, waited until she drove off, then assaulted me.
He tried to say it was consensual.
Of course they didn't buy it.
For once, the words on their forms matched what my body was felling: he was arrested for violating the order, and the charges that followed were the kind you don't confuse with a "misunderstanding."

The system finally had the right words on a their report.

Did he get charged? Yes.

Did I want them to pursue all of them? Yes. Then, I thought of his kids and got it dropped to a lesser charge, Under the conditions of him leaving me alone.

I do need to say this, because people love to ask the clean question: *Why didn't you shoot him?*

I wanted to. Believe me, I REALLY wanted to.

My hand was already in the glovebox, closing around the handle, and in that exact second my whole childhood fired across my brain like a flash, fear wasn't a normal response, every time violence was "just how it is," every time I learned to survive it was "it is what it is." Conditioning.

And then it was like God asked me one question "*Is that what you want to become?*"

After that thought it wasn't about him.

It was about what the system does when the "crazy woman" after someone has spent years making sure, she looks unstable, dramatic, hysterical. After he's trained everyone around her to roll their eyes before she even opens her mouth.

I knew the second I pulled that trigger; he'd get to become the victim.

And I'd become the headline.

I didn't put the gun down because I forgave him. I put it down because I refused to hand him the ending where he wins twice.

That was the day I decided to sell my guns.

I'd spent my whole childhood being cast as the problem—too damaged, too "crazy."
And I knew if I ever used a gun, even in the most justified situation, the world wouldn't see context.

They'd see this headline.
They'd see crazy lady "finally snapped."
They'd see my dad—the violence I came from—like it was stamped into my blood.
They'd see the villain they were already comfortable believing I was.

So, I sold them—not to protect him, but to protect me from becoming the ending people wanted to write for me.

With this entire situation there may be a report that doesn't mean the danger's over.

That's not how it works.

He didn't stop. He just changed his attack route.

CHAPTER TWENTY-THREE

The Hero I Gave Birth To

***

$\mathcal{J}$t was a couple years and still no peace. The kids and I attempted to start over somewhere else.

I ended up moving back to the area.

Cardboard boxes with tape.

Starting over again.

Knowing I was free but didn't have freedom from Glenn.

Anyone I met or tried to move forward with was in danger or threatened once he found out.

I sure didn't move back because I miss the town. And I didn't forget what it did to me.

My kids were suffering in the new school—real suffering, the kind adults minimize until it breaks something in them

Levi's seventeen now, was losing chances of a scholarship in the new school with the consumption of nepotism and Sarah was being picked on for being different.

I couldn't win.

So, I moved back.

And of course, Glenn treated that like an invitation.

He didn't come knocking like a normal problem. He came through my paycheck at first.

I was working at a factory then, and factory girls love to gossip.

He knew exactly what to feed them.

So he started calling my job. Calling people I worked with.
And suddenly he wasn't only in my phone, he was in the break room.

He turned my coworkers into his messengers— whether they knew it or not.

To make it stop, I tried to cut off his supply.
I didn't react. Gave no explanations. Had no conversations in the break room.
I showed up, worked, and went home.

But he didn't need my reactions.
He had theirs.

He'd call, drop a lie, and let it spread through my coworkers like it was their favorite kind of entertainment.
And I was the one standing there trying to breathe through it for eight hours.

I did what survival looks like when you're outnumbered:
I made a choice based on endurance, not pride.

And for a minute, it worked.
It wasn't the whole "I changed" line, I wanted him to feel like he was winning.
That's what people don't get.
Sometimes "going back" isn't love.
It's a hostage negotiation.

And hostage negotiations don't end clean.
They just buy time.

That "minute" of quiet didn't come with healing.
It came with a price tag—my dignity, my sleep, my

ability to feel safe in my own head.

And even when he got what he wanted, he kept his hands on the controls.

So, nothing after that was one clean event.

Nothing was a neat "then everything got better."

It was just a string of continuous disasters that—on paper—could look like proof that I'm a magnet for instability.

I'm not going to pretend I'm a perfect person once again

I made choices I'd make differently now.

There's a difference between "I made mistakes" and "I had control."

Because I was still dealing with a man who had mastered control.

A man who used every angle he could reach — people, rumors, cops, friends, timing, fear.

He didn't only show up. He managed the environment around me.

So yes, disasters happened.

And yes, I blamed myself — because that's what my I always tried to do:

If I can make it my fault, then I can fix it.

But I wasn't dealing with a fixable situation.

I was dealing with a person who treated my life like a game he was determined to win.

I once again moved to another home and this time was standing my grounds and was done no matter what it took because my kids weren't children anymore, they were grown teenagers with minds of their own

And finally, he made a mistake.
he didn't suddenly grow a conscience.
Time moved forward.
My son got older.
The little boy who used to need bedtime stories became a grown man with eyes and a brain and a body that could step into a hallway and say:
Enough.
Glenn barged into my home for the last time
Like always.
Like the door still belonged to him.
And he came down the hall toward me like he was going to do what he'd always done — attack, control, intimidate, prove that my "no" was still just a suggestion.
But this time my son was there and he didn't know it.
Levi.
Now eighteen.
Old enough to finally see the pattern clearly.
Old enough to understand what was really happening.
Old enough to stop being manipulated by the story. Glenn had been feeding him for years.
He stepped up.
Not with a speech.
Not with drama.
With presence.
With that kind of calm strength that makes a an abuser hesitate

And that was the moment everything shifted.

I wasn't standing alone in the hallway trying to stay alive and act normal at the same time.

For the first time, someone was standing next to me who didn't owe politeness.

Someone who didn't care about Glenn's reputation.

Someone who wasn't going to be impressed by charm.

That's when I learned a truth that still hits me in the chest:

Sometimes your rescue doesn't come from another man you date.

Sometimes it comes from the child you raised.

I got another PPO.

This time, it didn't just exist on paper like a polite suggestion.

This time, it had enforcement — because Levi enforced it.

Sure I had to file a show cause to prove the violation

He went to jail.

Many times, after that.

Because once my son understood the truth, Glenn's favorite weapon — doubt — stopped working.

Yes, the harassment didn't magically end.

There were still drive-byes.

Still little stunts.

Still the town slams but it got less as things became present not just by my eyes but my sons too. And the

side-eyes and the whispers like I was the one who
caused the scene instead of the one who survived it.

There were still moments when my life felt like it
was being tested on purpose.

But I could finally live.

Because I wasn't alone anymore.

People love to talk about "a man protecting his
family."

They love that story.

It sells

But no one prepares you for how it feels when the
one person who comes from you, the one thing you
made in this world — becomes the protector no one
ever was for you.

How it feels to finally have someone in your corner
who isn't charmed, isn't scared, isn't confused, and
isn't willing to play nice with a threat.

My hero wasn't just another man.

It was my son.

His quick mind.

His strength.

His ability to see through the bullshit and move like
its chess instead of emotion.

And the greatest feeling I could ever have wasn't
revenge.

It wasn't winning. It was this:

Feeling protected without having to beg for it.

Feeling believed without having to prove it.

Having the one thing that came from me finally
stand between me and the world like:

"I know who you are. I know what you did. You're not touching her again."

I owe him everything. And to this day, he watches out for me.

Quietly. Consistently. The way real protection looks — no speeches, no performance, just presence.

But I didn't see what was coming next.

Because life wasn't done testing me.

And the next thing that hit us didn't come wearing Glenn's face.

It came wearing something else.

Something I couldn't file a PPO against.

CHAPTER TWENTY-FOUR

The Last Lever

***

*Y*ears later, one last lever still existed—and he finally pulled it. He had patience and watched that calendar.

By the time she turned eighteen, Glenn didn't need access to me anymore, he found access through her.

By then, we were living our version of normal — school schedules, groceries, and the hope that the past would stay in the past.

People think once a kid hits adulthood, the danger shifts into something clean and legal and simple.

It doesn't.

It just changes shape.

Glenn played on her instability. On her soft spots. On the parts of her that wanted to feel chosen, protected, and grown all at the same time. Because he'd been circling our lives for years, he didn't have to learn her. He already knew the angles.

She was secretly talking to him.

Without my knowledge.

That's what men like him do best—he builds a separate reality inside someone's head, then acts shocked when you don't understand it.

The day she walked out the door to go live with him, she said something that split me in half:

"He's more of a dad than my real dad."

Then she yelled *"you're crazy and a liar"*

That I was trying to hurt him.

That I was the problem.

Sounds familiar?

And it was like watching him climb into my life wearing my child's voice.

He sheltered her like it was pride—like he was "saving" her.

But it wasn't protection.

It was grooming.

It was possession disguised as support.

I fought like crazy to prevent it.

Not politely.

Not calmly.

Like a mother who can feel the ground shifting under her family and knows exactly who's pulling it.

It was nonstop battles.

With her.

With her brother.

With her dad.

And every time I thought:

Okay, this is the part where a normal adult sees what's happening and steps in.

His friends stepped in first — on his side — like a well-trained dog

She left.

She didn't talk to me for weeks.

Weeks is a long time when you're a mother.

Weeks is a long time when you're sick with fear.

You can't drive over there and drag your own child

back without becoming the villain in the story he's already written.

In that silence, my mind did what it does best when it's scared:

It blamed me.

I failed her.

I raised her wrong.

I messed up so bad she ran right into the arms of the worst man I ever let near us.

This is my fault.

It's all me.

That was the soundtrack in my head.

Because if I could make it my fault, I could pretend it was fixable. I could pretend there was a simple correction that would rewind everything.

But the truth was uglier:

This wasn't about parenting.

This was about control.

And he knew my daughter was the last lever he had left that could move me.

Then out of the blue, she came back.

Just... back.

Like a door reopening.

I remember looking at her like I didn't want to breathe too hard in case she disappeared again.

I asked her what happened.

If she'd tell me.

If she could explain it in a way my heart could survive.

She didn't give me everything right away.

Not then.

But things started leaking back into the world —
like they always do in small towns.

My face went hot when I heard the version they
were telling. Only this time, the rumors weren't just
about me.

They were about my daughter.

And of course, the story in town wasn't: *A predator
isolated a young woman.*

The story was the same lazy script they always use
to punish mothers:

"She's crazy."
"She ran her kid out."
"She's the reason her daughter left."
"She's lying."

I heard versions of it that made my stomach turn.

While people were talking, I was calling.

I called the cops.

I called everyone.

I tried every "proper channel" I was told to use —
like channels matter when someone's running your life
through a smear machine.

I'm not proud of all of it.

It's not a polished "strong woman" montage.

I was frantic.

I was raw.

And there were moments I sounded exactly like the
"crazy" version of me he'd been selling — because
panic doesn't sound composed.

When you're a mother trying to get your child back
from someone who has been grooming them for
loyalty, you don't get to choose how you come off.

You just try to get them home.

That was his last strand of control.

The last way he could still pull me.

Then — finally — he crossed a line that even my daughter couldn't unsee.

She sat me down one day, after she'd been back, and showed me the messages.

Texts from him.

Threats.

Promises to destroy her life.

The worst part wasn't even what he said, it was why.

Because it wasn't really about her.

It was about me.

If I didn't come back to him, he was going to make her pay.

That hit me in a place unknown to me, that could still break.

Because I could survive him hating me.

I could survive him targeting me.

But using my child as a weapon?

That's a different kind of evil.

That's the evil that takes all the air out of the room.

And the second those messages existed —in black and white — something shifted in the everyone also.

People who had been sitting on the fence finally climbed down.

People who had been "not wanting to get involved" finally got involved.

Because it's one thing to dismiss a woman's words.

It's harder to dismiss screenshots.

It's harder to shrug when the threat is typed out like a confession.

And this time, I wasn't alone.

Not fully.

Not anymore.

The town that had been his weapon started turning into my support system — piece by piece, person by person.

Not everyone. Not magically. Not all at once.

But enough.

Enough to give me something I hadn't had during the worst of it:

Confidence.

Witnesses.

Mental support.

People standing around me like a wall instead of standing around me like I was entertainment.

And once I had that, I could finally fight back the way the system pretends it wants you to fight back:

PPOs that got enforced.

Jail when he violated them.

Calls that didn't get laughed off.

People who stopped treating me like I was "overreacting" and started treating him like what he was.

I already had the hero I never expected — my son.

Now I had something else I never expected:

A medium town — flawed, late, but real — finally surrounding me with the strength I needed to stop surviving quietly.

Then — like life wasn't done surprising me—

an angel appeared.

Not the cute kind with wings and glitter.

The kind that shows up right when you're exhausted and out of options.

The kind that changes the direction of the whole story.

CHAPTER TWENTY-FIVE

No Ties

***

After a couple years of being alone on purpose,
peace didn't feel like loneliness anymore, it felt like
home.

Stopping didn't look heroic. It looked small, plain,
and overdue.

I stopped.

I stopped dating.

I stopped trying to "figure it out."

I stopped auditioning men like I was the casting
director for my own next disaster.

I sat isolated in my house and kept building myself
back.

Not with grand speeches. Not with epiphanies.

Just quiet.

With routine.

And peace that feels suspicious at first — because
your body is so used to "hell's life" it mistakes calm for
a setup.

Here's the last thing I had to teach my body: calm
can feel like a setup until you practice believing it.

My son graduated and moved into his own place
with his own family.

And that did something to me I can't explain
without getting emotional in a way I hate:

It made me feel like I'd finally done one thing right.

My daughter finally enjoyed being a teen.

Not surviving. Not dodging adult problems. Not getting yanked into messes she didn't ask for.

Just being an eighteen-year-old — laughing, dressing up, getting dramatic over normal things. The dramatic that's supposed to be harmless.

I didn't see anyone serious

I started going to concerts with my best friend Tonja, The wild crazy type of friend who doesn't just hear you, she listens. And I listened to her dating disasters like it was live entertainment. I laughed, shook my head, and thanked every molecule in my body that my life was finally boring.

And during that time — while I was "finding myself"— I did go to counseling.

That's not a sentence I ever thought I'd say like it was normal.

Because healing was never something I was allowed to do.

Surviving? Yes.

Recovering? No.

Counseling made me discover a lot about why my life became such a disaster — why I kept ending up in situations that looked like different men but felt like the same pattern.

But it also made me discover something else, something I didn't even know was possible:

Healing.

Actual healing.

Not the "I'm fine" kind.

The kind where you start realizing your brain isn't you.

It's what happened to you.

That realization is both freeing and brutal, because once you can name it, you can't unsee it.

I had moments I wanted to run from everything.

Not run like "go for a jog."

Run like "disappear."

But I was locked in my own head by that old rule:

Never expect anything good because it always goes away.

That belief wasn't a personality trait.

It was a survival strategy.

A way to stay ahead of disappointment.

A way to keep my heart from getting its teeth kicked in again.

I'd had men tell me, "You deserve better."

Men tell me I needed pampered.

Men tell me they could "give me the world."

Every time, my mind would answer the same way:

That's not in the cards for me.

Like I had a deck of life, and somebody already stacked it.

Like "better" was something other women got.

Like my job was to be grateful for whatever didn't kill me.

Counseling didn't magically erase that voice — but it did something important:

It made me recognize it as a voice.

Not a prophecy.

Or God.

Not the truth.

Just an old program running in the background, trying to keep me safe by keeping me small.

So yeah! I got comfortable being alone.

Not lonely.

Comfortable.

Because no ties meant no mess.

No ties meant I wasn't handing anyone a handle to steer my life.

It went like that for a couple years.

And I loved it.

Because peace is addictive once you finally realize you're allowed to have it.

Then one day my son twenty-three years old, came over talking about a coworker I "just had to meet."

He was excited. Like excited-excited.

He said this man had taught him his job, took him under his wing.

I sat there listening to Levi talk about him like he was describing the dad he never had.

Not the biological dad. Not the complicated dad.

The version of a dad who shows up with consistency, guidance, and no agenda.

"He's amazing."

"He's solid."

"You would like him."

"You need to meet him."

I was like:

Nope.

Not doing it.

When you've rebuilt yourself from ashes, you don't casually invite matches into your living room.

Being lonely wasn't me.

I wasn't looking.

I was enjoying life with no ties or surprises.

Surprises in my life? End in house fires and police reports.

So, I said no.

Firm.

"NO"

That night, my phone went off.

It was message.

I looked.

And there he was.

We were friends already.

Hmm, Thanks Levi.

Which made my stomach drop because the universe has a sense of humor I don't appreciate.

How did that happen?

And why did it feel like a trap even though nothing had happened yet?

I asked myself "is this a test?"

Because I didn't want another disaster.

I didn't want another man with a story and a smile and a hidden sickness underneath it.

I didn't want to lose what I'd worked so hard to rebuild.

I was scared to answer.

He didn't do anything wrong.

It was my pattern of replicating my dad.

And I realized something in that moment:

I had gotten so good at surviving that I didn't know how to stand still...

I'd built a life where I couldn't be controlled.

And the idea of letting someone close, even a decent someone, felt like handing over the keys to a door I'd finally learned how to lock.

But the truth is, I always did the same thing with every person who crossed my path:

I gave them the disclaimer.

The understanding.

My boundaries.

The "this is me, take it or don't."

It wasn't any different.

If I was going to respond, it was going to be on my terms.

Not from that broken girl that thinks attention equals safety.

But from a woman who'd finally learned that peace isn't something you wait to lose.

It's something you protect.

If I answer... I'm not answering to be saved.

I'm answering because I'm allowed to meet a person without it costing me my entire life.

What happens next isn't another disaster.

It's the first time I had to learn a brand-new skill:

Allowing something good approach me... without running.

Because my kids deserved to see me whole, not just alive.

Eric didn't show up as a miracle. He showed up as a person.

And so did I.

Is it really love?

Some days, yes.

Some days, it's just two tired people trying not to bleed on each other.

We keep choosing the middle—

the place where nobody has to disappear to be loved—

and where accountability has to exist if love is going to stay real.

And if this book has an ending, it's this:

my life didn't stop hurting.

I just stopped letting hurt be the one steering.

I stayed—

not because I'm trapped,

but because I'm finally strong enough to leave if I have to.

What the Outside Doesn't See

***

People read stories like mine and think the plot is trauma.

It's not.

The plot is what the trauma did to my settings.

The Girl That No One Claimed was the childhood—where my body learned rules before I learned algebra. Watch faces. Measure footsteps. Don't talk too much. Don't need too much. Don't make anything worse. You grow up like that, and your neurons starts treating danger like weather. You don't stop it. So, you prepare for it.

Now, When Hell Comes Back isn't "why did she end up there again?" like I forgot everything I lived through. It's the adult fallout of being raised in a world where safety could flip on you without warning. You don't walk out of that clean. You walk out trained. And trained people don't always pick the healthiest option; first they pick the option that feels survivable.

That's why "just leave" is the dumbest sentence people throw around like it's helpful.

Leaving isn't a speech. It's something you can afford. It's childcare. It's a place to go that won't get found. It's a job you can keep while your head is splitting open. It's packing your kids' world into boxes while still acting normal at school pickup. It's doing the math at 2 a.m. with a shut-off notice on the counter and your stomach in a fist. And in a small town? Leaving means your name becomes a story people pass around like entertainment—half the facts, all the confidence.

And that's where judgment really hurts.

Because people don't just judge your choices. They judge your *character*. They make it sound like you stayed because you enjoy it, like you went back because you're addicted to pain, like you're stupid instead of cornered. That kind of judgment doesn't "motivate" anybody. It shuts women up. It makes them stop telling the truth because the truth turns into a courtroom. It makes them pick silence over public humiliation, even when silence is dangerous—because at least the danger is private.

That's also why I keep proof.

Not because I like paperwork. Because I've watched my reality get rewritten. I've watched lies win just because they were said louder. I've watched people argue about what I lived, swearing they know, but was never around and witnessed nothing but still turned it into a debate topic with people. So, I keep documents the way a drowning person keeps air: not for drama— for survival. For sanity. For the moment someone tries to tell me I imagined my own life.

Here's what nobody sees while they're running their mouth from a safe distance:

A woman can be unraveling and still get dinner on the table.

Still check homework.

Still do bedtime.

Still wake up fast when a kid coughs.

That's not strength the way people like to romanticize it. That's necessity. That's what a mother looks like when she's holding two worlds at once keeping her kids steady while she's shaking in private.

So, if you want to understand this story—both books—look at the wiring, not just the wreckage.

The Girl That No One Claimed is the girl learning how to survive being unclaimed.

When Hell Came Back is the woman realizing that survival training followed her into adulthood and tried to pass itself off as "normal."

And then something finally shifted in me.

Not a glow-up. Not a quote. Not a soft moment.

A line.

A refusal to keep paying for someone else's comfort with my peace. A refusal to teach my kids that love comes with fear. A refusal to keep shrinking just so other people can stay unbothered.

That's what hope looked like in my life: ugly, stubborn, and loud enough to move me.

And when that happens—when you stop editing yourself to stay safe—people who like you quieter start acting like you're the problem. They'll say you changed. They'll say you're bitter. They'll say you're "too much." That's only opinion and it doesn't matter.

Healing was never meant to make me easier to handle.

Healing was meant to make me harder to harm.

I'm not aiming for perfect. I'm aiming for faster: seeing the trap sooner, naming it sooner, leaving sooner. I'm aiming for real.

And if there's one final truth, I've earned the right
to say, it's this:
    Whatever broke me didn't finish.
    It taught me how to see what's in front of me—
and how to walk away.
I'm not afraid to be alone.
I've lived in survival my whole life.

The most dangerous lie is thinking you have no
power, because once you believe it, you no longer have
it. — P. Johnson

www.ingramcontent.com/pod-product-compliance
Lightning Source LLC
Chambersburg PA
CBHW031036160726
47991CB00005B/1899